The Ideal of Reparation

THE IDEAL OF REPARATION

NIHIL OBSTAT

F. Thomas Bergh, O.S B.,

Censor Deputatus.

IMPRIMATUR .

Edm. Can Surmont,

Vicarius Generalis.

Westmonasterii,
Die 1 Septembris, 1921

THE IDEAL OF
REPARATION

By RAOUL PLUS, S.J.

Translated by

MADAME CECILIA

OF ST. ANDREW'S CONVENT, STREATHAM

LONDON

BURNS OATES & WASHBOURNE LTD.

28 ORCHARD STREET   8–10 PATERNOSTER ROW
W. 1 ————————————————————————— E.C. 4
AND . AT . BIRMINGHAM . MANCHESTER . AND . GLASGOW

PREFACE

WHO WILL MAKE REPARATION?

THESE pages are dedicated to those Christians whose eyes are open and who have a heart, to these alone and to no others. Those who are not resolved to be generous with God need read no farther.

This book is dedicated to those who have seen Christ crucified, the Church crucified, France crucified. It is not for those who have seen nothing of this triple crucifixion—apparently, such are to be found.

It is for those who, gazing upon this picture of death, have realised the necessity of some work of life; not for those who have gazed upon the dead body of their Lord, upon millions of the slain, mere lifeless bodies, without a moment's reflection, without a feeling of indignation prompting them, like Elias of old, to exclaim: *Quid hic agis, Elia?*—"What dost thou here, Elias? In the midst of these ruins, dost thou remain listless, indifferent, inactive?" *Et vos hic sedebitis?*

In his "Journal of a Convert" Van der Meer de Walcheren gives an account of a "Revival

Meeting" in London. Two ministers came from America; they hired the Albert Hall, where they addressed more than fifteen thousand men. One of these preachers invited all who desired to give themselves to God to come forward. Clearly his voice rang out: "Who will come to the Lord?" For some time the immense audience remained in anxious, impressive silence. Then one voice was raised: "I will." At once, from all parts that cry "I will," "I will," re-echoed. And while the people were slowly coming down the long flights of stairs and making their way to the front benches, the two missionaries, stretching out their arms to them, continued their exhortation: "Who will come to the Lord?" Thousands responded and the cry "I will" resounded continually throughout the hall.

We do not need these emotional scenes, more or less artificial. It suffices for us to remember the words of Christ: *Si quis vult venire*—"If any man will. . . ." We need volunteers, souls that offer themselves willingly and that are faithful to their engagements.

Lord Jesus, raise up these volunteers, souls that rightly understand the Christian life, and likewise the nature and necessity of Reparation, volunteers whose nobility of soul leads them to give themselves wholly according to their state of life. Already there are many such, but the number must be doubled, trebled, nay increased tenfold. The world will be saved when we have a sufficient number of souls devoted to Reparation and not before.

Will anyone offer himself? Many devote their energies to objects far less noble, but none offers such hidden glory, such imperative urgency as Reparation.

Si quis vult venire—" If any man will. . . ." Who is willing?

Here am I, Lord, *I will*. Enlighten and strengthen me. Already, I am won over to Thy cause. Lord, I will.

INTRODUCTION

IN WHAT REPARATION CONSISTS

TO *repair* means to put a thing in good condition again. When a house becomes dilapidated and uninhabitable, it has to be repaired or *restored*. Sometimes the damage utterly destroys an object. In this case, reparation means *compensation*, giving the equivalent.

In the moral sphere, the equivalent, the ransom for injury sustained, can only be given by the oblation of one's self. No material object can adequately compensate. How can order be re-established? By some penalty inflicted upon the wrong-doer or self-imposed. Having allowed himself an unlawful and unbridled pleasure, it is just that some pain, duly proportioned, should re-establish the moral equilibrium. This is self-evident, without our discussing theories arising from the problem of God's vindictive justice. In this case, the equivalent of the wrong done is called expiation and, as in the preceding examples, can be offered by the guilty party himself, or by one, guiltless of the crime, who offers himself as surety.

In this book and in the Christian meaning of

the verb, " to repair " has a triple signification: *restore, compensate, expiate.* Having once stated these facts, we will now briefly explain:

I. *Why* Reparation should be made.
II. *Who* ought to make it.
III. *How* it should be made.

CONTENTS

CONTENTS

PART III

HOW REPARATION SHOULD BE MADE

PART I

WHY REPARATION SHOULD BE MADE

Because it is—

1. *A fundamental obligation of Christianity.*
2. *The formal wish of our Lord.*
3. *An imperative necessity, given the circumstances.*

CHAPTER 1

REPARATION IS A FUNDAMENTAL OBLIGATION OF CHRISTIANITY

WHY did Christ come upon earth? To make Reparation; for no other reason. He came to repair His Divine work which sin had ruined, to restore to man his supernatural life; to compensate, by His merits, for the insult offered to the Father in the garden of Eden and for those insults which man's malice daily renews and multiplies. He came to expiate by His sufferings—in the stable, during His Hidden Life and on the Cross—the human selfishness which began with man's creation and never ceases.

Our dear Lord could have performed this work of Reparation alone, but He did not so will it. He has chosen as associates each one of us, every Christian. We must grasp this truth well, for it is the foundation of the doctrine of Reparation.

St. Paul, when speaking to the early Christians of their pre-eminent dignity of sharing the very life of the Son of God, tells them that as Jesus lives by the Father, so they live by Jesus; He shares that life in virtue of His Divine nature, they in virtue of their adoption. He is their Head; they are the living members, who, in virtue of His Sacrifice, possess a Divine life. They are " divinely naturalised." Union is only perfect when the members are united to the head and the head to the members. The Person of Christ is the Head, they are His members, His Mystical Body.

Hence, according to the teaching of our Lord —" I am the Vine, you are the branches "—and that of St. Paul, the Catholic Church teaches that the *personal* Christ, consisting of the union of His Divine and human nature, such as, of old, He lived in Bethlehem, Nazareth and Jerusalem, such as He now lives in the Holy Eucharist, such as He lives and will live in Heaven until the end of time, does not constitute the *whole* Christ. He has willed it thus. The *whole* Christ consists of Himself—the Head, *plus* ourselves, His Mystical Body. Our intimate union with His Life explains why our Lord has associated us so closely with His work of Redemption.

Yet, as we have said, our Saviour could have perfectly accomplished it alone. He does not need us to add to His merits, but He wills to make use of us, that He may increase ours. He is *the* Christ; we Christians are each of us *alter*

Christus—" another Christ." We must work together. The Redemption will only be brought about by the will of our Saviour — the first Christ, and of all Christians those *other* Christs. Undoubtedly, His participation and ours differ immeasurably. His has an intrinsic, infinite value and is, of itself, infinitely sufficient. God could have dispensed with our co-operation, but because He loves us, He asks for it.

At the Offertory of the Holy Mass, the priest first puts wine in the chalice. Then, under pain of mortal sin, he has to add a few drops of water. Thus, our Lord's rôle and ours are symbolised, together with the proportional value of His action and ours. The wine alone would suffice for the validity of the Consecration. Nevertheless, the drops of water must be added, and by the effect of the Divine words of Consecration, they are changed, as well as the wine, into the Precious Blood.

Granted, our part in the Redemption of the world is infinitesimally small; what are a few drops of water ? But God requires it and He transubstantiates this tiny addition by uniting it with His own offering. This mere nothing becomes all-powerful, in virtue of the power communicated to it by God.* Thanks to this " nothing " which has become " something," souls will be ransomed. Without the offering of this

* Every comparison requires some modification. The few drops of water are not required for the validity of the Sacrament, but for its licitness.

" nothing "—so intrinsically insignificant and yet so really precious, on account of our union with Christ—many souls would probably be lost. The world needs all its potential saviours: it needs Jesus, its chief Saviour, its Saviour *par excellence;* it needs each one of us, who are called to co-operate with Him in the redemption of the world. As Lacordaire says: "The human race had perished as a whole, by men's solidarity, that is to say by its corporeal and moral union with Adam its origin. Hence, it was fitting that humanity should be saved in the measure and manner of its loss, that is by the means of solidarity. Where the solidarity of evil had lost all, by the solidarity of good, all has been re-established." (Conférence LXVI., *De la Réparation.*)

We are almost ignorant of our greatness as Christians, if we do not know our obligation of sharing in the work of Redemption. If we try to shirk our part, we are omitting a most noble, as well as a most peremptory, duty.

But we must examine this matter more closely. *How* did Christ make Reparation?

By suffering.

Here a problem confronts us. The Son of God, desiring to renew His work, to restore all to its primitive condition, *instaurare omnia,* was not obliged to choose a plan of redemption which would involve for Himself a life of suffering, pain and humiliation. Yet it was precisely this plan that He chose, rejecting all others, because He willed to repair all by suffering.

16

Whence it follows that, as we are necessarily united with Christ in His mission, since we form His Mystical Body, so we must necessarily co-operate with Him in His sufferings or " Passion." Therefore, St. Paul when explaining the necessity of our co-operating with Jesus in His work of Redemption, goes straight to the point and tells us that we must " fill up those things that are wanting," not in the *mission* of Christ, but in His *Passion* (*Adimpleo ea quæ desunt passionum Christi.*—Col. i. 24). The two unite, neither can exist alone. We must make Reparation with Christ, and we can only do this by uniting our sacrifice with His.

Bossuet writes : " In order to become the Saviour of men, Jesus Christ willed to be a Victim. But since He has a Mystical Body, it follows that if the Head is immolated, all the members likewise must become living victims " (*Serm. pour la Purif. de la Ste. Vierge*).

Here is the progression—we might more correctly say the equation—be a Christian, a saviour, a victim.

Nor is the term " victim " something strange or new. This doctrine is as old as the Gospel. It is the very foundation of the preaching of St. Paul, of the early Fathers and of the Church in all ages. The Apostle, in his Epistle to the Romans, sets forth this doctrine very clearly. He writes : " I beseech you therefore, brethren, by the mercy of God, *that you present your bodies a living sacrifice, holy, pleasing unto God* (xii. 1).

We cannot be true Christians and at the same time strive to lead a comfortable life, hoping at its close to pass quietly, without any shock, from a world in which we were very well off, to a heaven where we shall be perfectly happy; a heaven that is to be the reward of a life in which practically our chief anxiety has been to leave to others the laborious task of co-operating with Christ in redeeming the world. No, indeed, such a programme is incompatible with the Gospel of our Divine Master. His programme is totally different; it consists in the " terrible seriousness of human life," as Bossuet calls it.

Van der Meer de Walcheren, in the Introduction to his *Journal d'un Converti*—mentioned in our Preface—speaking with his usual bitterness, which is for once fully justified, says: " I am well aware that there are many so-called rational animals, who seem to live sixty or eighty years and are some day buried without ever once emerging from their nothingness. . . . Appearances were enough for them, all else had no existence." " Happily," he adds, " there are some real men, some who are really alive, and who have not received their souls in vain."

Shortly before his conversion, he says, referring to the same subject: " I am more and more stupefied at seeing the majority of men living on so calmly, not troubling themselves in the least about anything whatever. They wear a fat, self-satisfied smile, never giving a thought to *the yawning depths about us.*"

WHY REPARATION SHOULD BE MADE

Yes, deep abysses surround us: that of man's sin, that of God's love. God has placed the latter close to the former, and we stand between the two with our rôle clearly and imperatively defined. It is characteristic of the true disciple of Jesus Christ that he has found out these abysses and, in consequence, lives in an irrepressible anxiety for the salvation of the world, both on account of the sterility of the Precious Blood and of his share of responsibility in the story of the Divine life upon earth.

All Christians are under two obligations: First, they *must make Reparation* in union with Jesus Christ, who came upon earth solely for this purpose and, with whom, they form one unit. Secondly, they must make this Reparation *as He wills* —namely, *by suffering.*

Too few of the faithful have the faintest conception of the Christian life; they seem to imagine that practically there are two doctrines taught by our Lord, or at least two ways of interpreting His one law—one consisting in trying to suffer, the other in striving not to suffer at all; one of deliberate mortification, the other of deliberate avoidance of whatever is irksome. Briefly stated, they believe in an easy-going, comfortable kind of Christianity destined for the majority of Christians, whereas the other kind of Christianity, austere and crucifying, is reserved for those stern characters or fantastical people who feel drawn to it.

They find it quite natural that a priest, such

19

as the Curé d'Ars, a Saint, should write as follows:
" Everything reminds us of the cross. We ourselves
are made in the form of a cross. Balm and sweet-
ness exhale from the cross. The unction, which
overflows from the cross, inundates our souls,
in proportion as we unite ourselves with it, holding
it tightly against our hearts. The cross contains
more wisdom than any book; all who do not know
this book are ignorant, however many other books
they may have studied. Those only are truly
wise who love and consult this book, who study
it deeply. Bitter as this book is, they are never
happier than when they can immerse themselves
in its bitterness. The more they frequent this
school, the more they desire to remain there,
never do their studies weary them."

In a noviciate of the Franciscans of Mary, in
Canada, on one occasion six religious were wanted
to go to China to take care of some lepers. There
were forty novices, and all the forty volunteered,
each eager to have that honour. Some Christians, hearing this, remark coldly: " It is their
vocation." The very examples which should
arouse these lax souls and convince them that
they are bound to do something, if not as much
as these nuns, only serve as specious pretexts for
justifying their inaction.

They argue thus: Monks and nuns remain in
prayer all night, prostrate before the altar, or
rise for prayer at two in the morning in order
that we may sleep on comfortably in a good bed.
They pass their time in prayer in order to dispense

us from this exceedingly disagreeable task. They deprive themselves of food, therefore we can allow ourselves every luxury. They live in white-washed cells, furnished only, like those of Carmelites, with a crucifix, a holy water stoup, a death's head, and a discipline, so that we may adorn our houses with numerous ornaments and every modern comfort. If these religious go without fires, it is to allow us to have an excellent system of heating and a pleasant temperature in our rooms and passages. They sleep on a plank or a straw mattress, that we may have silken eiderdown coverlets and embroidered counterpanes. Their only jewelry is the cross, therefore we can wear trinkets and pearl necklaces that cost a fortune.

Undoubtedly, the perfect life exacts an amount of suffering, for which an ordinary Christian life does not call, but can we imagine any truly enlightened Christian life—even an ordinary one—that in any way harmonises with the feverish and pagan pursuit of the comforts of life, which modern materialism tries—and, unhappily, too often with success—to impose upon so many of Christ's disciples?

What then! Is Christ, perchance, divided?— *Nonne divisus est Christus?* Are there two Christs? Is there a crucified Christ, whom we can only serve by our crucifixion, and a restful Christ, whom we can manage to follow quite well while partaking of all life's joys and pleasures? St. Paul did not preach two Christs. He knew of One only,

" Christ crucified "—*Christum et hunc crucifixum*
(I Cor. ii. 2).

Men have changed this since St. Paul's time.
Now they know of two. The first, the true Christ,
did not suffice, so they invented another, one
without a cross, or a crucifying doctrine, a Christ
without those two beams which cast such a dis-
quieting impressive shadow, a Christ whose
demands amount to this: Live as you please; I
promise you a happy eternity, provided that
" you turn to me in your last moments with your
darkening mind, that you repent with your
failing will and give me the alms of your last
breath."*

There is no such Christ as this for Christians
who will not suffer. The disciple is not greater
than his Master. Our Saviour has suffered,
and every Christian must suffer in some form or
other—as we shall explain—if he would not
prove false to his name, or fail to accomplish his
mission; he must always and necessarily be the
friend of suffering.

A great Belgian statesman took for his motto,
" Rest elsewhere." The day of perfect happiness,
perhaps not far off, will surely dawn, perhaps
soon, and will have no sunset. Meanwhile
time is given us that we may merit " the joy of
the Lord." *Intra in gaudium Domini tui.* But
we can only enter into the joy of the Lord on
condition that upon earth we have shared the

* Philippe Gounard, killed in the War. *Réflexions et
Lectures*, pp. 204, 205.

22

sufferings of our Lord. Christ was the first to choose suffering as the way into glory. " Golgotha is not a rhetorical flourish." For us too the same rule holds—*oportuit pati Christum et ita intrare in gloriam suam.*

We wish to triumph with Him, therefore we must fight with Him. In the *Exercises* of St. Ignatius, in the Contemplation on the Kingdom, the Saint places these words on our Lord's lips: *Laborare mecum.* Pizarro, a conqueror of South America, disembarked and threw his sword upon the ground to mark off the bravest, and called out: " Let all who are afraid remain where they are, let the others cross over and follow me."

This is stern language, and in spite of the convincing force of the doctrine many draw back rather than face the suffering which is the inevitable consecration of all Christian life.

" How those two arms of the Cross frighten me, as they stand out on the hill of Calvary ! I feel more inclined to hide behind them than to be nailed upon them !"

" Yes, the wood is hard; but there is something more than the wood. There is One nailed to those arms. The wood is dead, but a living One is fastened to it. Looking at the Cross, as we ought to look at it, we no longer see the two arms, they disappear or at least become indistinct; the Body hanging there, alone rivets our attention and, in the midst of this Body, shining through an open wound—the Heart. We say: ' the Crucifix.' We are wrong: for we appear to name a *thing*. We ought to say: 'The Crucified,' for that shows a person."

" A person? Yes, in truth, a Person who is both human and Divine. What! Is it Thou, my God, who hangest there?"

" Yes, It is I."

" Now I seem to understand better, I almost grasp the truth: I will suffer with Thee, Lord, but Thou wilt suffer with me. With Thee, I shall be brave and march resolutely forward."

" That thou mayest have still more courage stand at the foot of My Cross and look round upon the world. Look at My executioners as they go down the slope of Calvary; look at Jerusalem, wrapped in slumber, where the multitudes know nothing. Thou must suffer in order that My Redemption may avail them. I have willed that thou shouldst help Me. I can do all with thee and nothing without thy aid. Wilt thou that we save the world together? Or dost thou prefer to go away along with all the crowd?"

" Art Thou really speaking to me, Lord? Surely, Thou knowest not who I am!"

" Thou art one of Mine own. Is that not enough for me to ask thee to work, suffer and endure with Me? The task is immense as thou seest. But I assure thee that it is worth the price, though it involve the oblation of thyself as a living victim, in union with Me, even in thy present state of life."

" Dost Thou think I can? A living victim along with Thee, O Lord? Ah, yes, with all my heart—take me!"

CHAPTER II

OUR LORD WISHES US TO MAKE
REPARATION

THE necessity for our making Reparation is logically deduced from the very foundation of our Catholic Faith and, in particular, from the doctrine of the Mystical Body of Christ, and that of the Redemption. It is likewise shown to be an imperative duty from the long, formal, and constantly reiterated chain of instructions given by our Blessed Lord.

Whether we open the Gospels, or examine the great revelations handed down to us, we constantly see our Lord setting forth His great desire to find souls capable of suffering, utilising it for the glory of God and the salvation of souls.

Let us turn first to the Gospel. There are numerous texts which teach the obligation of doing penance as an act of Reparation; no law is more frequently inculcated.

Our Master chose St. John the Baptist as His precursor. What did he preach? " The baptism of penance for the remission of sins " (St. Luke iii. 3). What does he continually repeat, day after day, on the banks of the Jordan, where Jesus Himself was soon to commence His ministry? " Do penance, for the kingdom of heaven is at hand " (St. Matt. iii. 3). How does he live? As an example: " John had his garment of camel's hair . . . his meat was locusts and wild honey," his abode " the desert of Judea " (*ibid.*, ver. 4). How does he answer those who came to him asking " Who art thou ?"— " I am the voice of one crying in the wilderness : Make straight the way of the Lord." Men had made God's path crooked; it had to be made straight again : this is reparation.

What a well-merited rebuke he gave to those hypocrites who came to ask for the baptism of penance, without any intention or desire to lead a better life ! " Ye brood of vipers. . . . Bring forth fruit worthy of penance. . . . The axe is laid to the root of the trees. Every tree that doth not yield good fruit shall be cut down and cast into the fire. . . . Hasten, for there cometh One; He is even now among you, and you know Him not. If He finds good wheat, He will gather it into His barns, but He will burn up the chaff with unquenchable fire."

Is it possible to set forth, in a clearer or more thrilling manner, the necessity of suffering as an act of expiation, the obligation of returning to the straight path, of atoning for past faults, of imploring pardon by offering some proportionate penance ?

Afterwards our Blessed Lord Himself appeared in public. He commenced His ministry by fasting in the desert for forty days. When He called men to be His Apostles, He bade them leave all and follow Him, and exhorted the crowds that surrounded Him to deny themselves. St.

Matthew significantly remarks: " From that time, Jesus began to preach and to say: Do penance, for the kingdom of heaven is at hand." St. Matthew seems to point out that from the very beginning of Jesus' Public Life, He preached on the theme so dear to Him and so constantly reiterated in His discourses.

Moreover, our Lord extolled suffering and expiation for sin all His life. He taught men to give one coat to the poor if they had two; not to trouble about what they should wear; that money was to be despised and heavenly treasures alone valued. He constantly anathematised those who loved the broad road, and ever strove to lead men to walk in the narrow way. He predicted untold woes to the rich and to hypocrites. He taught men that the truly blessed are those who are poor and gentle; those who weep; those who thirst for justice, who are merciful, pure in heart; those who are peacemakers, and who suffer persecution. Such is His doctrine! " Are you willing," He asks, " to follow Me seriously? Then, as a preliminary step, you must deny yourselves and embrace the cross with both hands: nothing less will avail."

Our Lord does not restrict His teaching to words: had God merely given maxims or pre-cepts, He would not have been understood. He reduced His words to actions, " The Word was made flesh." That which had hitherto reached only to the ear became visible to the eye: precept became example. Jesus lived His whole life upon earth as a Victim, that He might give us an example and teach us how to suffer.

As soon as He came into this world—*ingrediens mundum*—how did He explain His life's work? *Dicit: hostiam et oblationem noluisti. Tunc dixi: ecce venio* (He saith: " The victims of the past thou wouldest not; then said I: Behold, I come ").

In the womb of Mary, Jesus only began His apprenticeship for the victim's life He was to lead later on in the confinement of innumerable tabernacles. Jesus was born; and in the manger, in the stable, in Bethlehem, He was still a victim. As Tertullian writes: " He was a Victim from the virgin birth." From his birth onward, His sufferings continued; He endured the Circumcision, the Flight into Egypt, the Exile there— nothing was lacking as regards suffering. Hence, in His Public Life, Jesus could say " Blessed are those that suffer;" " Blessed are the poor." How these words would have provoked resentment, had He been born in luxury! But He was the most destitute and afflicted of all.

In Nazareth, He lived a hidden life. Had He not done so, men would never have accepted the doctrine of humility which He preached afterwards. As it is, in spite of His example, how few trouble about His doctrine! Men love to be seen; He effaced Himself during thirty years. A ransom was required to atone for men's pride, so Jesus lived a hidden obscure life of painful toil. Holman Hunt, in his celebrated painting " The Shadow of the Cross," represents our Lord stopping work, standing up, and stretching out his arms to ease their weariness. The light flings His shadow back upon the blank wall, which is horizontally divided by a shelf from which hang some carpenter's tools. The effect is striking. It is that of a man's form standing out in relief from a cross.

During His Public Life, Jesus, wearied and footsore, tramped the roads of Palestine in search of souls. He was thirsty and asked the woman of Samaria for a drink; He spent nights in prayer; unceasingly he exercised His ministry. Foxes have their holes; birds, their nests; but the Son of Man had not where to lay His head, not a roof to shelter Him. He had to make Reparation for all those who pursue vain things, and worship the golden calf; for the children of God who either forget or deliberately neglect to pray to Him; for the sowers of evil seeds, and for those in whom the good seed remains sterile. When Jesus began His Ministry, what name did the Baptist give Him? " The Lamb of God who taketh away the sin of the world." John meant: Here is the silent Victim for all men who will save the world. Throughout three years, Jesus with Divine patience endeavoured to impress upon His Apostles that the Christ must be delivered up to His enemies. They could not understand His words; their meaning only dawned upon them when, from their hiding-places in Jerusalem, they saw Him afar off nailed to the Cross on the summit of Calvary.

29

But above all, Jesus stands forth as our Victim in His Passion. Then, because He so willed, He was betrayed, denied, insulted, buffeted, outraged and nailed to the Cross. Thus He willed to teach us to suffer in our body, our affections, our reputation and our honour. He suffered likewise, because Divine justice required some compensation for all those who only live for pleasure, who betray their baptismal vows and their Faith, for those who deny the Faith, who mock at the Passion and persecute Christ's disciples, for those who scoff at the Church, the Pope and priests—in a word, for all who, in their shameless egoism, find the Cross of Christ so irksome. Christ so much loved Reparation that He glorified it in Mary Magdalene, once publicly known as a sinner, who became in " Mary of Bethania," where He called her to Himself, a model of repentance and love, and afterwards Mary of Golgotha. At the foot of the Cross there were but three—you will never find many where there is suffering to endure—three only, one man and two women—Mary, John, and the Magdalene—between two who had never lost their innocence, one with innocence regained at the price of generous expiation through a twofold breakage, her broken vase and her broken heart. To such a degree was her soul purified, that she was the first, after our Lady, who was privileged to see the Risen Saviour on Easter morning.*

* *Reparation* is commonly used in the sense of compensating *for others*. Clearly this does not exclude the

WHY REPARATION SHOULD BE MADE

We have seen how greatly our Lord values Reparation; leaving the Gospel, let us now turn to the great revelations handed down to us in the history of the Church. What do we learn from those of Paray, Lourdes, la Salette, Pellevoisin, Pontmain?

In the revelations made to St. Margaret Mary our Lord's one object appears to have been to ask for Reparatory sacrifices. Let us take a few examples from her life: On one occasion Jesus said to her: " Behold the Heart, which has so loved men and in return only receives ingratitude and contempt. That is why I ask thee to make Reparation."

The Saint tells us: " The Sacred Heart wills

---

idea of expiating one's own faults when one has committed any, and one's own " indelicacies " which one is never without. We may note an instance of the pain felt by a truly loving spirit at the thought of its least daily shortcomings in the account of *Sister Gertrude Mary* by the Abbé Legueu (p. 99): " I feel quite sad at the thought of loving our dear Lord so little. How grateful I am to you for showing me my indelicacies. ' Indelicacy ' towards our Lord is a word that touches me very deeply. It has wounded me to the quick. I don't mean, I am annoyed by it. Oh, no: I am very grateful to you for it, but I want to tell you that I feel how much I am constantly grieving our Lord. . . . O dear Jesus, in return for all the love Thou dost lavish upon me, I give Thee nothing but indelicacy and ingratitude." After that we are not surprised at our Lord saying to her: " My Child, bestow upon Me numbers of little attentions." (The account is taken from *Une mystique de nos jours*. Angers, 1910.)

31

that souls should make Reparation by returning Him love for love, and that they should humbly implore pardon of God for all the insults that are offered to Him."

Again, Jesus said to her: " My daughter, it is true that My Heart has sacrificed everything for men, without receiving from them any return. I feel this more acutely than the torments of My Passion. In spite of all My eagerness to do them good, they treat me with coldness and contempt. Give Me the pleasure of making up for their ingratitude."

In 1669 in the month of February, at the time of the Carnival, St. Margaret Mary wrote to the Rev. Mother de Saumise: " The loving Heart of Jesus seems to make me this request, namely, that I would stay with Him, close to His Cross in these days, during which all rush madly after pleasure, and that by the bitterness, which He will make me taste, I should, in some measure, compensate for the bitterness with which sinners immolate His Sacred Heart. He wishes me to grieve unceasingly with Him to prevent sinners from filling up the measure of their guilt."*

In order that Reparation might be made by devout souls, our Lord asked for a special feast to be instituted in honour of His Sacred Heart, for the Communion of Reparation on the first Friday of each month, and at other times for this same object; and for the practice of the Holy

* *Vie et Œuvres de la B^se M.-Marie*, par Mgr. Gauthey, t. ii., p. 425.

Hour. Most of Christ's instructions to St. Margaret Mary tended to train her—and through her ourselves—in a spirit of Reparation.

This is what He asked of her for the Holy Hour: " Every week from the Thursday night to the Friday morning, I will cause thee to share in the deadly sadness which I allowed to overwhelm My soul in the Garden of Olives. Thou wilt rise between eleven o'clock and midnight and remain prostrate flat upon the ground for one hour, that thou mayest satisfy the Divine justice, by imploring mercy for sinners and likewise, in some measure, mitigate the sadness I felt when my Apostles abandoned Me and could not watch even one hour with Me."

It is impossible to misunderstand our Lord's meaning. The first time the Sacred Heart appeared to this Saint on December 27, 1673, He was seen upon the altar, the chosen place of sacrifice, with the face of one in pain. He asked her to draw a picture of His Sacred Heart, with the wound made by the lance, surrounded by a crown of thorns and surmounted by a cross. Hence we can well understand the fiery utterances of St. Margaret Mary. She exclaims: " If only you knew how our Sovereign urges me to love Him with a love that will share His life of suffering! I know of nothing that is more fitted to ease the tiresomeness of our lives, than patient endurance with love. Let us suffer lovingly without complaining and count as lost all moments passed without suffering." The whole life of this Saint is one hymn of Reparation, of love that begets conformity to His suffering life. It is useless to give copious citations from her life or works, they must be read through.

The Rev. Père Terrien in his well-grounded book on *Devotion to the Sacred Heart*, says: " To make Reparation is to love, but above all to suffer, to sacrifice self through love "* (T. iii., ch. iii.).

" It is in the Heart of Jesus that we obtain the precious supplement of love, which alone can render our reparations really pleasing to Him."

Jesus knocks at the door of our heart, asking us to make Reparation, but our poor alms have no value unless they pass through His Heart. There is a blessed ebb and flow of the tide of love, it originates with Him and invites us, and our love must return to that centre if we are to correspond effectually with His advances.

David said that he had found his heart that he might speak to God; we can do better than find ours, seeing that we have the Heart of the Son

* This love does not, however, take away our instinctive horror of pain. Thus we find our Lord saying to Saint Teresa: " My daughter, thou askest Me for suffering and then complainest when I send it. . . . Nevertheless, I answer thy prayer considering thy set will and purpose, rather than the natural repugnances of thy nature " (*Life of St. Teresa*). Mark well the words *thy will*. It is a question of will and not of feeling. True piety, the piety that makes reparation, has nothing to do with feeling. This truth should be printed at the foot of every page of this book.

34

of God. St. Bonaventure's sole desire was to dwell therein. He pitied the blindness of those who do not know how to find entrance into Christ, through His open wounds, especially that of His Heart.

We then will say: "*Introibo ad altare Dei*— I will enter humbly, but resolutely, even to the altar of my God." In the Office of Lauds the Hymn for the Feast of the Sacred Heart says in substance: "O Heart, symbol of Christ's passion of body and soul, as a Priest He offered in thee His twofold sacrifice. Who would not venerate and love thee? Who would not choose thee for his dwelling-place for ever?" This holy sanctuary of His Heart, where Jesus continually renews His Sacrifice, shall likewise be mine: there I will offer my humble share in His work of Redemption. How can I do this? By striving to unite my sentiments with those of His Adorable Heart, in conformity with the spirit of the Apostleship of Prayer, which is one of many methods and ranks with the best.

But what are the sentiments of the Sacred Heart? Consider first His "*Ecce venio!*"—Lo, I come, I offer, I give Myself. The whole life of Christ is one prolonged "Ecce," one unceasing ratification of the immolation of His first day. *Ecce Rex!* on Palm Sunday. *Ecce Homo!* on Good Friday. *Ecce Agnus Dei!* There is our Lord on the banks of the Jordan and in the Eucharist. Mary, the most faithful of all His imitators, had her "Ecce" likewise. *Ecce an-*

cilla !—" I offer myself, I give myself up to Thee "
—was her unceasing prayer.

Two ardent desires continually flow from the
Heart of Jesus. First, He is consumed by an
insatiable thirst to do the Will of His heavenly
Father; secondly, He thirsts continually for the
baptism of blood which is to save us from eternal
death. Now this twofold desire extends, in
Jesus, to all that constitutes Jesus.

It is indisputable that in His personal Humanity,
our Blessed Lord can no longer humble Himself
or suffer. But we constitute His Mystical Body,
and He desires that each Christian should give
himself wholly to the fulfilling of God's will.
The Sacred Heart desires each one to offer those
Acts of Reparation which have to be united to His
own Sacrifice. If Jesus can no longer humble
Himself in Himself, He can do so in us, for we
are one with Him. This is why He asks for our
share and our offerings.

Alas, how few understand His appeal, how few
accept ! Nevertheless, all true devotion to the
Sacred Heart goes as far as this. It even constitutes its very essence and those who interpret
it otherwise either diminish or distort it.

In the Eucharist, Jesus is with us under the
form of the " host," *i.e.*, victim, thus clearly
expressing His ardent desires. Under the species
of the Sacrament, our Lord does not actually
suffer from the indifference, irreverence, immorti-
fication, pride, revolt and sacrilege of men.
But when He trod this earth He foresaw all these

36

and suffered unspeakable tortures on account of these insults and outrages offered to the Divine Majesty and from man's horrible neglect of God's laws. He foresaw every single sinful act and atoned for each in detail.

He asks us to console Him now for all His Sacred Heart suffered in those hours of trial; He wills that, by our piety, we should make Him some compensation. Since He has chosen to perpetuate by the Holy Eucharist the Sacrifice which He consummated upon the Cross, how can we better satisfy His desire than by continuing His sacrifice as He Himself does—*i.e.*, by becoming victims in union with Him? And since, in this Sacrament of love, Jesus still mystically hungers unspeakably and suffers an unquenchable thirst to accomplish the Will of God and save souls, what can we do better than enter into the sentiments of the Divine Guest of our tabernacles?

We shall emphasise this point farther on, when explaining the nature of the love for the Blessed Sacrament which should animate a soul devoted to Reparation. Let what has been said suffice for the present. When we rightly understand true devotion to the Sacred Heart, our Eucharistic life becomes the union of two hosts or victims in the union of one perfect oblation; and when we truly grasp the meaning of our Eucharistic life, that is of our union with Jesus as Victim, our devotion to the Sacred Heart then becomes practically one sustained effort of self-renunciation in order to become a living " appearance," under which Christ alone lives. We aim at becoming a living " appearance," that He may use us as an instrument to continue the accomplishment of His Divine work; a living " appearance " that is unceasingly sacrificed with Him in the unity of the same sacrifice for the glory of the Adorable Trinity and for the salvation of souls.

We have dwelt somewhat on the revelations of Paray le Monial and the devotion to the Sacred Heart because they bear on the subject of Reparation. This holds good of the great apparitions of our Lady in France—to mention only those of the nineteenth century. In all these it seems as though their sole object was to remind men of the need for Reparation. To Bernadette, our Blessed Lady expressed her grief at the invasion and flooding of the world by sin, and as some compensation, she asked that men should pray and do penance. She told Bernadette to recite the Rosary and asked that a church should be built at Lourdes in which God would be glorified by the public homage of the ardent acclamations of countless pilgrims boldly vindicating their living faith in an age characterised by blasphemy and forgetfulness of God. Above all, she insisted upon the necessity of doing penance, saying sorrowfully : " Penance, penance, penance."

When she appeared to two children at La Salette she urged them to pray and do penance. She told them sorrowfully that God was about to chastise men severely unless they prayed and did penance. She mentioned blasphemy and the desecration of the Sabbath as the two sins that especially cried to Heaven for vengeance.

What are we to learn from all this? The need of souls—souls devoted to reparation. God is saddened by men's sin. It will fare badly with us if there are not voluntary victims forthcoming to fling into the other scale of Divine justice their sacrifices to God.

CHAPTER III

REPARATION, AN ACTUAL DEMAND OF TO-DAY

THE more sterile the land, the greater is the call for labour. Morning and night we pray "Thy kingdom come," and yet what is more self-evident than the fact that our wish is still unrealised?

Who would dare assert that God's kingdom has come? Is it not only too manifest that God's kingdom has not come and that we see no signs whatever of its advent?

Péguy places on the lips of St. Joan of Arc some words which fittingly describe the sad state of things at the commencement of Charles VI.'s reign, words which can truthfully be said by us in our days: "Our Father, who art in Heaven, how far, far off is the hallowing of Thy Name, how far off the coming of Thy Kingdom! The world is worse than ever. If only we could see the sun of Justice rise. But, O God, forgive me for venturing to say it, Thy Kingdom seems to be going farther and farther away. Never has Thy Name been so blasphemed nor Thy Will treated with such contempt. Never has man been so disobedient. We have not yet enough saints upon earth; send us as many as we need, as many as are necessary to dishearten the enemy."

Huysmans, in his admirable Introduction to

the Life of St. Lydwine of Schiedam (d. 1433), gives an outline of the state of the world when God chose Lydwine for Himself. When skating one day she was knocked down and broke her ribs. Gangrene set in, and for thirty-eight years she endured intolerable sufferings both in soul and body. She was chosen by God to keep Satan thus in check, and to hinder the daily increase of his kingdom.

Has the world changed much since the times of St. Lydwine? In her days men killed one another. Our age can vie with that of those older barbarians. Nations were crumbling to dust in decrepitude and decadence, men were willing bond slaves of paid sophists and false shepherds without a conscience. Have we not seen this also? Money to bribe traitors was plentiful in those times. Is it not always at hand? There are philosophers in abundance, now as then, ready to excuse the greatest atrocities.

Love of pleasure reigns universally. "In a few days, I shall be twenty-three. It is time to enjoy myself." This motto chosen by Beyle has been practically followed by whole generations. Sin displays itself with such disconcerting cynicism and abundance. One hardly knows where to stop when giving examples.

In an article entitled *Panem et circenses* (Bread and the show of the circus)—the cry of the populace of ancient Rome—Monsieur Reverdy gives statistics of the amounts realised in 1915, the second year of the War, by the principal pleasure centres in France, such as theatres, cinemas, smoking concerts. The total amounted to 22,880,000 francs. Of this sum the theatres received 8,000,000 francs, the cinemas 7,000,000, and the concerts and music-halls netted the rest. " Thus nearly twenty-three millions of francs (about £1,120,000 sterling) were spent on pleasure by a country in the throes of war, and in which few families had been spared bereavements in War victims. This is rather a large sum." " Large " indeed ! It is neither more nor less than monstrous. Yet while our Bishops and all who are zealous for the moral purity of our streets protest against the display of bad books and suggestive pictures, there are actually men who clamour for " room to be found for free and easy behaviour and moving voluptuousness and even—why not ?—for the indulged sensualism so often found in so many of our French literary masterpieces."

Then behind these open vices are all the faults that are sheltered and hidden.

" Lord, may Thy Kingdom come ! Alas ! How far off it still is !"

Out of one thousand five hundred million human beings, there are only five hundred and twenty million Christians : of this number, only two hundred and sixty millions are Catholics, the rest are schismatics or Protestants. The remainder of the total consists of Jews, infidels and pagans. Yet the dear Lord shed His Blood for all !

Alas ! We lack Apostles. Twenty-seven centuries ago the prophet Amos uttered this strange prophecy under the sycamores of Bethel: " Behold the days will come, saith the Lord, and I will send a famine into the land; not a famine of bread, not a thirst of water, but of hearing the word of the Lord. And they shall move from sea to sea . . . they shall go about seeking the word of the Lord and shall not find it " (viii. 11). It is the same now; although Christ has come, the nations sit in the shadow of death.

A tribe in Central Madagascar had been deprived of their pastor. He was needed elsewhere, for there was a dearth of priests. This is what the deserted flock wrote to his Superior: " A terrible misfortune has happened to us. We are like men who have been suddenly plunged in utter darkness through the extinguishing of their torch. The torch of the Catholic Faith had shone upon us and made us supremely happy. Alas! How sad is our fate now! Help us, Father, hear our cry of distress; we are like sheep without a shepherd, the sport of wolves. Send us back our priest."

True devotedness to the cause that we espouse means a great deal. It entails the service of our mind and intelligence and above all of our heart. It means loving the cause we are eager to further so much, that we are prepared to sacrifice ourselves wholly together with our tastes, preferences, habits and inclinations and not merely a given portion of them. It means loving souls so ardently that we go in pursuit of them, without

43

waiting for them to come to us, without looking for their love and gratitude in return, but devoting ourselves solely for the love of God and of souls. Such self-devotedness is by no means easy, and this is why the world in desolation clamours for it. The source of Divine grace is ever within reach, ready to gush forth in living streams and to cleanse men from sin, to purify conscience, give sight to the blind, heal the leper and the paralytic, but volunteers are needed, as at the Pool of Bethsaida, to bring God's help to succour the misery of humanity.

Valentine Riant used to say: " If devotedness is required, I am ready." She accepted generously the call to consecrate her life as one act of Reparation for the abominations and vile crimes of the world. But how few have the courage to imitate her example!

After the siege of Paris in 1871, Rénan and some of his friends had a gold medal struck, bearing an inscription which ran thus: " During the war, some people used to meet at Brébant's every fortnight, and never once noticed that they were dining in a city numbering two millions of the besieged."

It is ever thus. The world contains two classes of people: the few who, like that generous victim of Reparation, have eyes to see and intelligence to know what is passing around them, and who are so affected by the sight, that they are forced to give their assistance, and the others who, imitating Rénan, the egoist, and his associates—

and their name is " legion "—see and understand nothing, or if they by chance obtain some inkling of the truth, take no heed. In the midst of a world that is hurrying on to destruction, they think only of feasting at the restaurants of their times. In any case, they give no thought to the millions of unhappy beings around them, creatures who are enslaved by wretchedness, doubts and want of God. We all know Carlyle's caustic remark about the " Eighteen millions, *mostly fools.*"

As we are so accustomed to live in the midst of egoism which prevails and rules everywhere, we do not perceive the hatefulness of this vice. Those whom some special grace has enlightened in their darkness of unbelief outside the Church, and led them suddenly to the clairvoyance of faith in the Gospel, are full of astonishment and contempt for the " nobodies " who fill the world and want nothing beyond the vanities which satisfy their mean desires.

The Dutch artist, Pierre Van der Meer, in his " Journal," owns that while on his way to faith he is amazed at seeing the utter indifference of some people, and they are the majority.

He passed through the City of London, " that mournful region of trade, money and business. . . . From every door, street, corner, by-place and blind alley, gentlemen were dashing out, dressed in black and hatless. They all rushed in the same direction and apparently to the same place. A Japanese Loan had just been floated, the subscription lists were open. Evidently, there was money to be won, and like savages they dashed after their prey."

Another time, he reached Paris by the express which arrived at six a.m. He writes: " On the Boulevards Rochechouart and Clichy, I witnessed the joys and sorrows of the preceding night. The chandeliers were still alight in a large room on the first floor of a café. Presently I heard the shrill harsh laugh of some girl. I met men and women in evening dress. With drawn tired features and dull eyes they were hurrying home on foot or seeking for some conveyance."

Elsewhere, he sees men who simply live to eat. Speaking of one he says: " This glutton certainly has no fear of death, nor does he concern himself unduly with the mystery of life. What can be the life of the soul in such an individual ?"

Again he writes: " An old American lady boards in our hotel." She boasts of having neither relatives nor friends. "Yet," she said, " all the same I have one unique friend; here it is," she added, as she threw down her purse on the table.

Consider two other examples of a worldly life. A young girl lay on her death-bed and just as she was expiring she said to the nun, who was nursing her: " Sister, my hands are empty."

An Austrian nobleman, a relative of Count Czernin, as he lay dying, said: " When God asks me to render an account of my life, what shall I answer ? I can only say: Lord, I have killed hares and hares and hares, and nothing more.

It is really too insignificant," and he spoke the truth. We are no partisans of Jansenism, no enemy of lawful amusements, but we condemn the terrible habit of looking at life from the sole point of view of how much pleasure it can be made to yield. There is something else to do.

But we have not yet touched bottom. Men might at least be contented with neglecting God as is the case with the majority, but some go further. For them, it does not suffice to ignore God, they are animated by a most virulent hatred of their Creator and of the Catholic Church.

We were justly stirred up to anger and resentment by the sacrilegious fury of our enemies during the War against our churches; but was not a book entitled *La Grande Pitié des Églises de France* published long before the War?

Yet, after all, material monuments are little compared with that great spiritual temple—the Catholic Church which is the Bride of Christ. How does the world treat it? We need not go far back in order to catch the echoes of menacing, inimical words in our public legislative assemblies.

Here are a few examples: " In 1905 or 1906 at the latest, Catholicism will be dead and buried." " I mean to put an end to this clerical reaction, three months will do. I need no more." " This is what you would say, O Catholic Church, but you no longer have any life in you." " The Church is falling to pieces." These sentiments were expressed as recently as 1903, 1904, 1906 and 1908.

Active measures followed upon these words, innumerable Acts against religion were passed. Thousands of the best disciples of Jesus Christ, torn between their patriotism and their Faith, had to go into exile. They alone know what great sacrifices this involved.

Look at that marble tablet placed over the entrance to a home for the aged. After the monks had left the Carthusian Monastery of Neuville, near Montreuil-sur-mer, the civil authorities made the building into an alms-house for the aged, and on this marble tablet in golden letters (well befitting the words, forsooth !) this inscription is inscribed:

" The sad and solitary life hitherto led in this cloistered monastery has disappeared for ever. It has given place to a free and open life, active and fruitful for the progress of mankind. With the works of the past, we construct the works of the future."

This inscription is a quotation from the discourse delivered at the inauguration of the alms-house.

In France we have had divorce laws, " Priests turned into Tommies," and general laicisation. Then came the laws of association, decrees to put us outside the law. And now we have Separation and the Inventories. And where is Jesus Christ in all this ? And where are His teaching and His Vicar and His ministry, and His chosen disciples ?

We yield to none in honouring our beloved

country. But let us not imitate the pharisaism of those who refuse to acknowledge her mistakes. For the sake of her future let us make honest admissions.

Réné Bazin, writing during the War with his usual delicacy of expression, sets forth the anomaly of a crucifix—which for years had occupied a place of honour in the schoolroom—being found by some American soldiers in the school-mistress's attic. The crucifix had been relegated to the rubbish heap! Surely such an act of vandalism helps to explain how a conversation such as the subjoined could take place. Two children were in the Museum at Cluny looking at a large crucifix: " Look, Madeleine," said one, " does not *that man* look wretched ?" " Why does he hang down his head ?" " He seems to be crying, don't you think so ?"

Yes, poor little ones, indeed He weeps; He weeps because you do not know Him. He sheds tears because some of your own family have prevented your knowing and loving Him.

What meanness there is in these attacks against Religion, be they open or secret! Formerly our coins bore the inscription " God protects France." This glorious sentence has been suppressed and it is considered a disgrace to name the Master of the Universe in a public speech or an official document.

God! Why He no longer exists! One public statesman has grandiosely declared that " All the stars are extinguished." Another

speaks of himself as "God's personal enemy."
Jaurès, the greatest advocate of laicisation, in
an eloquent discourse that concealed assertions
no less blasphemous, made the subjoined state-
ments in the Chamber of Deputies on February 11, 1895:

"We must before all safeguard the priceless
treasures acquired by man in spite of so
many prejudices, sufferings and combats. These
treasures consist in the realisation of certain
principles, namely that there is no such thing as
revealed or sacred truth; that all truth which
does not spring from man is but error; that
even when we give our adhesion to certain
principles, our critical faculty must always be
on the alert. Further, that a certain aggressive
mental attitude should underlie all that we think
and affirm, that even though our ideal of God
should take shape or if God were to manifest
Himself to men under a tangible form, our first
duty would be to refuse Him our obedience, to
treat Him as an equal with whom we discuss,
not as a master to whom we submit."

And God sees all that: He hears all that!
For whom do they take God? In vain do men
assert that God is nothing, in vain do they stand
forth and shake their fists at the sun and declare
"You don't exist." The sun still shines in the
heavens, and God still counts.

Vile degraded men who insult God and deny
His very existence, who leave Him on one side,
are powerless to injure the Most High. Those

who deny and insult must remain here below. Heaven is inaccessible to them. Earth, alas! is not and are we sure that these insults rising from our midst will not fall back in punishments upon us?

God is God; all those who would put out the stars and deny the supernatural are powerless; they cannot get rid of Him.

God exists—eternally. He, too, has His rights. God will not suffer man to treat Him as an outcast with impunity, as one who can be overlooked or got rid of; as one who can be disposed of by an eloquent discourse, a vote, or a stroke of the pen.

But if we cannot find enough volunteers to counterbalance all these insults, what may we not expect?

In Claudel's *Annonce faite à Marie* we find the subjoined passage: Anne Vercors, a farmer's wife of Combernon in the time of Joan of Arc, announces her intention of going to Jerusalem.

THE MOTHER: What! you are going away? For good? And where are you going?

ANNE (*pointing vaguely towards the south*): Yonder.

THE MOTHER: To Château.

ANNE: Farther than Château.

THE MOTHER (*in a low voice*): To Bourges, to see the other king?

ANNE: I am going to the home of the King of Kings, to Jerusalem.

THE IDEAL OF REPARATION

THE MOTHER: Good heavens! Is not France good enough for you?

ANNE: There is too much sorrow in France.

"Too much sorrow in France!" Yes, in very truth!

In the time of Abraham, two cities would have been spared if only ten just men had been found. And how greatly we need just men, how many more of them!

The Rev. Matheo Crawley, the well-known Peruvian missionary who has travelled all over France, has truly said, "For every social evil, I have found not simply one work of reparation, but a whole series of them."

If these good works are to flourish, we must have many, many souls of good will, souls eager to adopt a mode of life like that so aptly set forth in the subjoined passage:

"We must give up certain satisfactions and practise mortification because others are suffering, and do these things with the greatest sympathy, because we feel drawn to share their sufferings. We must deprive ourselves likewise of certain pleasures, because others indulge in them to excess. In this case, we wish to ransom or compensate for their immoderation. So far as our position and powers allow, we try to maintain a certain level in the life of men."

Send us, O Lord, we beseech Thee, many of the just to make compensation for their brethren. May it please Thee to send us not merely faithful souls of the rank and file, but generous souls pledged to pay by their loyalty the ransom which Thy justice has asked for so long. Suffering alone will not suffice: we need suffering welcomed—*devota et pœnitens*—loving and penitent suffering. There are other urgent needs but these are the most imperative.

But do yet more, dear Lord, raise up souls who, not content merely to accept suffering, seek and desire it as a means of restraining the power of evil. These are the souls who make reparation to the uttermost.

Cardinal Manning wrote: " We do not live in the age of martyrs (but, who knows?), but in an age when each must have the will of a martyr."

In a book written before the War, Daniel, the hero of the story, makes an excellent retort, which is likewise a rebuke, to a worldly young priest who was quoting with satisfaction the words of a bishop in China, who had witnessed many martyrdoms and speaking of them, said: " In my young days, I longed for martyrdom, but I do not want it now."

Daniel replied: " Let me tell you that if there are in France a thousand Christians, a hundred, or even twenty ready to suffer in their bodies the stigmata of the Passion, these alone are the true disciples of Christ and you may recognise them by their readiness to shed their blood joyfully. The earth on which we stand has drunk in their blood greedily, it was the blood of Sanctinus, of Blandina and of Irenæus.   If France is to be born again, our blood too must be poured out."

Yes " our blood too must be poured out." Not perhaps on the battlefield or in the arena, but it must be shed drop by drop in our daily striving after holiness, and for the restoration of humanity in Christ. It must be given drop by drop by the daily sacrifices—often so trivial and yet meritorious—of an existence spent wholly for God.

The most faithful of these zealous souls give all to God, making the complete sacrifice of their self-love with all its manifold reservations, of their most cherished attachments, of their most legitimate pleasures and joys. They give all for the joy of seeing God at last known, loved and served as He merits.

PART II

WHO SHOULD MAKE REPARATION

CHAPTER I

CHRISTIANS AND REPARATION

THE obligation of perfecting or filling up the mission of Christ, and consequently His Passion, falls more especially upon those who are called by God to consecrate their lives to Him, but we cannot draw the conclusion that the ordinary Christian has no part in this noble work. On the contrary, each of the faithful both can and ought to assist and, in the measure of his generosity, enter the ranks of those consecrated to Reparation.

The first reason for this, and one which should appeal even to tepid Christians, is *their own personal interest*. We all know the laws of Divine justice. We know that as surely as God exists and cannot cease to exist, so surely crime will not ultimately triumph, but, sooner or later, sin will meet with its due punishment. God punishes sin · sometimes upon this earth, but not often. He mercifully delays avenging sin in this world. After all, if man persists in his evil-doing, God can satisfy His justice in eternity. But peoples and nations, as such, have but a terrestrial existence and consequently must pay the penalty of their evil deeds in this world. Their punishment here in some form or other is inevitable. This truth is strikingly exemplified in the history of the Old Covenant. Listen to the words of Jehovah addressed to the perverse Hebrews by the prophet Jeremias:

" The Lord said to me: Behold I will call together all the families of the north . . . and they shall come, and shall set every one his throne in the entrance of the gates of Jerusalem and upon all the walls round about and upon all the cities of Juda. And I will pronounce My judgments against them, touching all their wickedness, who have forsaken Me . . . and have adored the work of their own hands" (i. 15).

Farther on we read: " Behold I will bring upon you a nation from afar . . . a strong nation . . . whose language thou shalt not know, nor understand what they say. Their quiver is as an open sepulchre: they are all valiant. And they shall eat up thy corn and thy bread: they shall devour thy sons and thy daughters: they shall eat up thy flocks and thy herds: they shall eat thy vineyards and thy figs. With the sword they shall destroy thy strong cities, wherein thou trustest" (v. 15).

Note that God often makes use of a wicked nation—as we learn from the history of the Israelites—to give a salutary admonition or fulfil a glorious mission. Nor need we confine ourselves to past history; the present age provides us with striking parallels.

Undoubtedly, we cannot apply this law to any one particular case: we cannot assert as a positive fact that Napoleon's exile and death in St. Helena was the expiation of his deeds at Savona and Fontainebleau, because the general law is one thing and its particular application another; and this general law is as follows: All crime must be avenged and God necessarily must triumph ultimately.

It is possible, looking at the Great War from one point of view, to assert—without committing ourselves to any paradox—that it was an act of mercy on God's part. On the other hand, it better fits in with the facts to look upon it as a punishment from God, as an act of Divine justice. But men, blinded by pride, refuse to admit this explanation.

A soldier wrote as follows: " On all sides, agricultural implements, pierced with bullets, lie rusting on the ground. Tombs with their crosses are seen everywhere, in the middle of farm-yards, in clumps of bushes, under trees. Tell me, is it not terrible to look upon *this vengeance of the Cross ?* When shall we understand it ?"

All who have gazed upon the innumerable cemeteries and thousands of tombs on the battle-fields have felt this truth come home to them: " Men had banished the cross from their public monuments, their Courts of Justice, their schools and highways. Yet behold, the simple wooden cross is seen on all sides in the woods, along our highways, even in the midst of our gardens."

What were men so eagerly seeking formerly ? What, alas ! are they still too often seeking ? Pleasure and enjoyment. Even in so many so-called Christian families, what licence is tolerated ! What contempt there is for the most stringent laws of God touching the sanctity of wedlock, the observance of the Sabbath and due respect for the good of our neighbours. All modern life is planned out with the view of escaping from suffering and from the inconvenience of complying with the binding precepts of God and of the Church.

Meanwhile, suffering bides its time, it prepares its revenge. Its hour came in August, 1914, when the War broke out. What anguish followed: there were separations, last farewells, constant anxieties. Weeks and months passed. Then news came: the loved one was wounded, a prisoner, or missing, or even worse than all these ! Poor suffering creatures ! What a capacity for pain there is in the heart of man !

None but those who were in the fighting line or on the vast fields of battle can imagine the amount of anguish, the multitude of sufferings that were crowded into certain hours, days, or even months of such an existence.

So much for the past, but what of the future ? What remains of so many human joys, happy homes and fair fortunes built up with such labour and trouble ? Can we remain untouched by the sad vistas that open out and the inevitable sorrows that are foreshadowed ?

Can we do nothing to remedy this ? Yes,

we can do a great deal. During the War, there were three great Armies—one to fight, one to nurse, and one to pray.

The army that fought paid its tribute to our country. It gave one million three hundred thousand lives. To their deaths, we owe our lives. The army of nurses showed boundless devotion. But perhaps the most powerful army, the one that most contributed to the victory, was the army of prayer and sacrifice, and to this belonged many of the soldiers of the two former.

St. Joan of Arc's words express a constant truth: "The hands that grasp the pike gain fewer battles than the hands lifted up in prayer." A grave writer has said: "The inexplicable victory of the Marne was perhaps won by the humble prayer of a little child. . . . See that poor girl praying in some ruined sanctuary. She knows one truth, that God ever hears our prayers, since He has promised to answer the petitions of those who trust in Him. Listen, it is night and you hear the endless rumbling of an army on the march—infantry, cavalry, and impedimenta. All this noise comes from the prayer of an innocent girl whom God will surely obey."

These supernatural influences certainly played a great part in the history of the War, between 1914 and 1919. What will be their share in coming events? As great and as glorious as we choose to make it.

It is only too manifest that society is in the

throes of a vast upheaval. Agitation prevails everywhere. Even more than in the past, the world has need of souls who are ready to ward off God's anger. Uneasiness and wild rumours predominate, convulsions rumble in the distance.

Would that we knew to what an extent we have it in our power to bring the Divine action into the sphere of our human history! For this, it is not necessary to give up natural means; we have to use them, but we must teach Christians—even those who have little faith in supernatural helps— that these play their part in modifying the course of human events.

He is powerful who acts upon the First Cause of all that is. Now the First Cause of *all*, in this world's history, cannot be *nothing*.

When St. Louis was setting forth on his crusade a violent storm arose. The saintly king knelt for some time in prayer, then rising calmly, he assured his companions that the flotilla would make the voyage in safety. " How do you know that ?" they asked. " Because," replied the king, " my monks of Clairvaux are praying and doing penance, so all will be well with us."

A few years ago someone asked one of the bishops of China which was the best means of obtaining the conversion of that immense Empire. " We must have some more Carmelites and some Trappists," replied the bishop.

Such means might seem totally inadequate for the required purpose, but we cannot go against the truth. What then is the truth ? Well, think what ruins souls—Sin. What saves nations? Holiness, and the two essential elements of holiness are prayer and penance.

From this follow two conclusions. First, we have to ask ourselves whether in our own lives in any degree, however small, we have ever contributed to bring about the state of things which we deplore so much. In certain Eastern countries, when a man has been murdered, the corpse is placed in some public place, and each citizen has to come forward in turn and, placing his hand upon the dead body, swear that he is innocent of the crime.

In presence of our country in such dire distress, we must not imitate Pilate and declare, as he did when judging our Lord, that we are in no way to blame for these evils. Can we say how far the effect of our sins may have reached? Had there been more just men in Sodom and Gomorrah, these two cities would not have perished by fire.

Let us keep from sin. "What overturns nations? Sin." (*Quod evertit nationes? Peccatum.*) (Prov. xiv. 34.) It is the sins of individuals which draw down misfortunes upon the people, far oftener than we imagine.

One single mortal sin *in itself* is sufficient to cause God to send some great calamity upon the earth. Very few understand this, and yet it must be said. For what is mortal sin? It consists in deliberately putting a creature in place of God, in ignoring Him, in desiring to do away with Him were such a thing possible.

61

Now of itself the annihilation of all that is finite could never make adequate reparation for an insult offered to the Infinite Being. These are the exact data of the problem, and whatever decisions men promulgate or accusations of cruelty they bring against God, the problem remains as before.

How many useful lessons we might learn even in our generation from the history of the chosen people of God, if indeed the men of our age could still take any interest in the subject. Take the subjoined example: When the army of Israel marched against Jericho, one of the soldiers was guilty of a great fault. God had said all the booty was to be reserved for " the treasury of the Lord "—*i.e.*, for sacred purposes. Disobeying this command, Achan, an Israelite, took from the spoils " a scarlet garment, exceeding good, two hundred sicles of silver and a golden rule of fifty sicles . . . and hid them in the ground" (Josh. vii. 21). The army of Israel were defeated. Someone had disobeyed the Lord. The Lord of hosts left Israel to himself. The transgressor had to confess his sin and expiate it. " Then," said the Lord to the Israelites, " ye have won the day "—not, ye shall win, but, " now ye have won the day." And in fact the Israelites then and there destroyed their foes.

Thank God, however, that under the New Law He does not often punish the masses for the crimes of individual persons. But, nevertheless, God can do so if He wills and in so doing He acts with perfect justice, since all the temporal punishments collectively cannot compensate for one mortal sin seeing that there cannot be any approximation between the finite and the Infinite. Yet God, in His mercy, permits that sufferings inflicted by Him or voluntarily self-imposed by the Christian shall have the power of expiating faults. As our Lord said to St. Margaret Mary: " One just soul can obtain the pardon of a thousand sinners." In this way, without infringing on the rights of justice, God is able to exercise His mercy super-abundantly. He frequently asks us to co-operate with Him to our utmost, so as to provide opportunities for Him to show His infinite mercy.

Our duty, then, is clearly marked out. We must not be scandalised, perhaps to the point of blasphemy, by occurrences that upset or distress us, as if we were amongst the pagans of to-day; we must not imitate the pharisaically faultless and self-righteous critics around us, who reject every explanation of historical events that accepts the principle of expiation. On the contrary, we must realise what sin really means and, in future, avoid it as the greatest evil whether for individuals or nations. It does not, of course, follow that given two nations, the most prosperous is necessarily the most holy, but the truth remains that theoretically—if not always practically—a mortal sin can bring the greatest calamity upon the world and, if we have any care for the well-being of society, our first duty is to lead a good life and avoid those deeds which God, in His justice, cannot do otherwise than punish.

We should do well to meditate on what Newman writes on this question; in the light of what we have just said, there is no fear of our mistaking his meaning:

" Let us not conclude that God makes use of other punishments to-day (than of old) because we do not see His direct action. The principal difference between the punishments inflicted by God on the Israelites and on Christians, is that the former were visible, the latter invisible— that is, we do not perceive these evils to-day as the chastisements of God, because God Himself or His chosen prophets no longer tell us this explicitly; but the effects of God's anger are no less real, and are even more terrible, seeing that they are proportioned to the greatness of the privileges which we have abused."

The task set before all Christians is not, however, purely negative. Each one, who desires to remedy or prevent sin, must place some counterpoise in the scale of God's justice. Alas ! how many sins are committed in our land ! For these, we must offer an ample measure of fidelity to prayer, acceptation of suffering and progress in holiness. Hence every Christian should make Reparation, from a motive of self-interest. If he evades this obligation, the whole Christian body, all civilised society, an entire nation, may have to expiate his want of foresight or sinful indifference.

But there is another and a nobler motive; not that of interest but *love*.

Is it possible to see God so insulted without feeling impelled to make Him some compensation ? Can we look on and see Christ our Lord, our Head, mocked at and treated as an outlaw without a feeling of indignation, of regret, or of deeper love for His cause ? It is true that, from the days of His Agony in Gethsemani and His Crucifixion, He is accustomed to have but few of His disciples with Him—but, even so, cannot we be of that number ? Where is the faith, where are the noble sentiments that should animate the souls of baptised Catholics ? Will none come forward to mitigate His sufferings ? Will none try to comfort the Church in her grief ? Are there only priests and religious who can realise what suffering costs and how much misery afflicts men ?

" Look around you and tell me whether the world is governed by the Spirit of God who created it, or by the spirit of Satan, the world's idol and destroyer ? We must make Reparation for all those who, though baptised by water and the Holy Ghost, have nevertheless sinned against Him. Yet we remain all the time indolent and inactive " (Manning).

The Holy Spirit is betrayed every hour of the day. Are there none willing to make Reparation ?

We see the Church of Christ continually attacked, now openly and shamelessly, now secretly and cunningly. Are we always going to remain inactive? During the battle of Eylau, Napoleon, seeing himself very closely surrounded by the enemy, called out to Murat: " Don't you see they are gaining ground? Will you let the fellows swallow us alive ?"

If we can remain so indifferent, it is because we do not love our Mother, the Church. The term " Mother " is an empty sound, a mere mockery. Shall we suffer our Mother to be insulted with impunity? Formerly, if anyone had grieved our human mother, should we not have striven to make amends to her by increased tenderness?

Mgr. d'Hulst writes: " We need in the world devout souls who love God and are desirous of making Reparation and of doing it without stirring up the resentment or curiosity of their neighbours by their choice of means." Thanks be to God, there are some, more perhaps than we think.

It is related that a poor peasant woman was nursing her dying son. Presently, the young man, half-opening his eyes, exclaimed: " Mother, give me some water, I am dying of thirst." At this moment the clock struck three. The Christian mother took a crucifix and, placing it in her son's hand in a voice broken by tears, said to him: " My dearest child, it is the hour when Jesus too was tormented by thirst and died for you upon the Cross. Won't you endure a little thirst to be like Him ?" " Yes, mother," replied the young man and, putting the crucifix to his lips, he kissed it tenderly. Unconsciously these two, mother and son, were animated with the sentiments of St. Francis of Assisi when he exclaimed: " What, Thou, my Saviour, art nailed to the Cross, and I am not nailed to it !" Their generosity puts these two among those " *good* Christians " of whom the saintly Curé of Ars once said: " Worldlings complain dolefully of having crosses; good Christians grieve when they have none "—amongst those who have understood what Fénelon calls " the great mystery of Christianity, that is the crucifixion of man " in union with the crucifixion of Christ.

True love ever begets imitation: this is the unequivocal mark of its genuineness. We subjoin a few examples.

Eugène Courtois, a member of the " Association Catholique de la Jeunesse Française," was killed in the September offensive of 1915. He was an honest workman, who had been converted by the example and influence of his dying brother. He practised great austerities, rising very early in order to receive Holy Communion daily, sleeping upon a wooden cross which he placed each night in his bed even when he had a deep wound in his feet, nor would he have his wound attended to, because he desired to suffer. He devoted himself to tending the sick, whose ailments were most repulsive. He was never happy except when suffering, and frequently complained that his food was too good and that he had not enough privations.

THE IDEAL OF REPARATION

Lucile X., when quite a child, happened to read the life of Sœur Céline de la Présentation, who died in the Convent of the Ave Maria at Talence. Lucile resolved to imitate her by giving herself up to a life of Reparation. She attended a Mission at Maubeuge, which strengthened her resolution. In December, 1902, she made her first Communion and four years later wrote thus in her spiritual note-book: "Jesus, I offer Thee the sacrifice of my life for my beloved country. . . . Make me suffer that I may expiate the crimes of France." In her piety and ardour all is genuine and practical. She writes: "Self-renunciation consists in doing my duty, no matter what it costs me and without troubling in the least as to what I prefer. If I have a choice of two things, I will choose the most mortifying and will sacrifice my inclinations and do what others wish. I will never show any preference for a given thing nor use the words 'I prefer.'"

What wisdom this girl shows; how she understood true self-renunciation! She knew herself well when she said to God: "Send me suffering. Do not listen if I murmur when Thou answerest my prayer. O Jesus, do not cease to send me suffering: I give myself wholly to Thee." The Divine Master ceased to send her trials when He called her home to Him on May 29, 1907.

The Curé of Ars used to say: "A Christian lives amidst crosses like a fish in the water."

Yes, provided he seriously follows the teaching and example of His Master.

Madame Elizabeth of France in the prison of the Temple prayed thus: " My God, I accept all, I will what Thou willest, I sacrifice all to Thee, uniting it with the Sacrifice of my Saviour." Général de Sonis prayed: " Let me be crucified, Lord, but by Thee." In the terrible fire that broke out in Paris in the Convent of the Sisters of St. Vincent de Paul, where a bazaar for their works was in progress, many fell victims to the flames. Among them was a young girl of twenty. In her half-burnt note-book, found on her dead body, were written these words: " O Jesus, I offer Thee my life as a ransom."

Little Bernadette Dupont asked God at her first Communion that she might become a religious and die a martyr. God did not answer the first petition, but accorded her the second. She died at the age of fifteen, after a painful illness of nearly three years.

Here is an example of a commanding officer. He was a Breton of noble birth. At one time he had almost decided to give up his military career, rather than sacrifice his faith. War broke out and he resolved to pursue it. Not content to remain in charge of home defence merely, he asked to go on active service. Passing by Domrémy he visited the sanctuary of St. Joan of Arc, where he uttered this generous prayer: " I offer my life as a ransom for so many young men who are not guilty of the sins of their

69

fathers." He felt that his offer was accepted by God. When placed with the third battalion of Zouaves, on starting out, he said to one of his companions: " The greatest honour of my life will be to suffer for my country." A few weeks after, he fell on the battlefield. The parish priest, his intimate friend, read the subjoined extracts from this brave soldier's letter:

" Does not our beloved country need voluntary victims, ready to offer themselves as holocausts for her ransom? If only God would accept me as a victim of expiation, as a ransom for our land, how gladly would I give my life for the sacred cause of Reparation." "After having seriously considered the matter and prayed earnestly, in spite of the sentiment of my utter unworthiness, I have ventured to offer myself." " I do not know if, in spite of my faults, God will judge me worthy. But should He mean to hear my prayer, I thank Him in anticipation for all His kindness and indulgence."

Mirabilis Deus in sanctis suis. It is indeed admirable what God can effect with such a wretched thing as the heart of man. Let us admire it and, at the same time, try to understand it. Many know nothing of such heroic acts: those who perform them, generally speaking, do not realise their own heroism. There are different degrees of generosity and greatness in these deeds, ranging from the most glorious to the most humble (which are not always the least meritorious). Those who have heard of these voluntary victims know that there are more than we might imagine. Doubtless, specially privileged souls retain their high place and are consequently not numerous, but, as the examples just cited prove, God has chosen souls even in the world and among those who live an active life.

We have already given Father Matheo Crawley's testimony to the religious vitality in France. We will now give another quotation from his works:

"The generation of Christians, ready for daily sacrifices and even the greatest, that of their lives, is still in existence. We must not look upon it as a thing of the past. In the great centres and in the villages, I myself have come in contact with chosen souls, whose moral beauty was absolutely surprising. But they must be sought for. Like the hidden springs of water, they work secretly and silently. Their hidden virtues spread fertility all round. Everywhere, in every rank of society, among those in high position, among influential men as well as among the obscure and humble workers, God has His chosen souls.

"Whence do these priceless souls spring? They are the drops of blood of a noble race, the voice of the living traditions of the old Catholic stock, the moral wealth of an organism that is steeped in the purest and most virile Christianity. It is of this wheat that God has kneaded

71

the reparatory victims (*nostras reparatrices*) of France."

It devolves upon us to cherish and guard these chosen grains of the purest wheat. If God has inspired us with the germ of generous desires, let us beware of the indifference that environs us. If we would be ready to suffer, we must love God. Is this so difficult?

On the 25th of Ventôse (the sixth month of the first Republican calendar), 1794, one of the judges of a revolutionary tribunal asked a saintly young girl—Marguerite de Pons: " What are your religious views?" to which she answered simply: " I love God with all my heart."

And who cannot make the same reply? Loving God with all our heart—that is equipment enough for starting on the work of reparation. That, too, is enough to keep us carrying it on successfully to the end.

CHAPTER II

RELIGIOUS AND REPARATION

"THERE are in the world some roads with never-to-be-forgotten names."*

One is the *Regina Viarum*, " the Queen of roads." Through Capua, Benevento, Brindisi and the Ionian Sea, it put Rome in communication with Greece and linked together the two poles of the world. It was the highway of artists and poets.

Another is the *Via sacra*. It skirted the Palatine, crossed the Forum and led up to the Capitol. It was the conquerors' road.

There is a third, the *Via dolorosa*. It starts from the citadel of Antonia—Pilate's residence, in Jerusalem—and runs by the houses of Annas and Caiaphas to the top of Calvary. This was the way followed by our Saviour, and still trodden by all who wish to walk in the footsteps of the Crucified—the Sorrowful Way, or in the words of the *Imitation*, the Royal Way: " The Royal Road of the Cross."

Is not the essence of all religious vocation a call to unite with Jesus Christ in a special way? By sanctifying grace alone God admits us to a marvellous intimacy, and we possess God in our souls. But if the title of " Spouse " can be

* H. Reverdy, *L'absence et le souvenir dans la guerre.*

applied strictly speaking to God, living in every one of the baptised, how much deeper is its signification when the soul is not merely engaged in the way of the commandments, but is chosen and marked out from all eternity for His special service, and is set apart by Him from the beginning, selected, attracted. and consecrated by Him.

Marriage consists in mutual engagements and the placing of the ring on the finger. Baptism can truly be called a marriage, since it consists of the union of God and the soul, but the term means far more when we refer it to Religious, those souls of predilection with whom God is so intimately united in virtue of their vow of chastity.

It is part of the essential condition of the state of matrimony that husband and wife form but one. They share together all their projects, joys, perplexities, anxieties, sufferings and trials. Their hearts are united and beat in unison.

If a Religious is in earnest, if the soul is truly the Spouse of Christ, this will be her prayer:

" Love for love, life for life, blood for blood, offering for offering: all is one between us. Thou canst no longer suffer, but Thou hast confided Thy mission to me, and with my whole strength I devote myself to this work. In order to make Reparation to Thee and to assist Thee in saving the souls for whom Thou didst offer Thyself, I will suffer for those who live for pleasure; I will love for those who blaspheme; I will be humble for the proud; weep for sinners who laugh, and give Thee my whole soul for those who reject Thee.

"I hear Thy complaint; I hear Thee say: 'My love is unrecognised and persecuted. I seek a place of repose and I have chosen thy heart.' Like Sister Elizabeth of the Trinity I will 'offer Thee a dwelling, a shelter in my soul, and there my love shall make Thee forget all the insults and outrages of sinners.' I know that in my soul in the inward 'temple' of Thy grace Thou wouldst see an altar of sacrifice for Thy divine transformations set up. I will offer Thee the matter of the sacrifice, which by Thy Divine presence and power, Thou wilt transform and divinise. Thou, in me, wilt offer Thyself to the Father and Thou wilt offer all without consulting me. Do not heed my repugnances nor resistance, suppress pitilessly whatever hinders Thy designs. Must I not 'be made perfect in one' in order to work efficaciously for all to be united with Thee? If Thou art not wholly in me, how canst Thou be my All-in-All?

"Dear Master, long ago, by holy Baptism, I received grace and Thou didst take possession of my soul. Henceforth, I possess Thee more intimately by my vows. Thou, by Thy power, wilt destroy in me all that is not Thyself. I yield up all my faculties to Thee. From now my path in the future is clearly traced out. My one aim shall be to repair the outrages committed against Thee by so many ungrateful sinners. In the rags of my spiritual poverty I will strive to devote myself to Thy service, and though a poor substitute for Veronica, I have but a worn veil and an unworthy heart, I will pass my life consoling Thee in Thy sadness, and binding up Thy wounds. I hold tightly the crucifix of my vows, of our reciprocal engagements. With Thy permission, I put my lips to Thy Sacred Wounds.

" I kiss the wounds in Thy hands as a Reparation for those who do wrong; I kiss Thy forehead, pierced by the thorns, as an atonement for sinners who think not of Thee, or only remember Thee that they may outrage Thee. I kiss the Wound of Thy Heart to atone for those who hate Thee and love evil.

" I would fain do more, for the truly devoted souls do more than say ' Lord, Lord !' I long to prove my generosity by my acts, by imprinting upon my life, if not upon my body, the sacred stigmata of Thy Passion.

" Assuredly, what I offer Thee is but little and insignificant. Yet one thought consoles me. It needs so little flour to make an altar bread, only a few crushed grains. I will resemble that altar bread which will become the consecrated Host. To remind me of its littleness, I will adopt as motto: ' He must increase, and I must decrease.' To imitate its whiteness, my ideal shall be the purity of the Angels, and in imitation of its immobility—for the Host is carried or

placed as the priest wills—I will obey unquestion-
ingly and instantly."

Such is the general outline of the spirit of
sacrifice of a fervent Religious. The consecrated
life in itself presupposes the acceptance of a
crucified life, but some chosen souls, desiring
to go further than their Rule obliges, aim at a
life of continual and great suffering—the greatest
possible. The desire of constant, radical and
unceasing immolation in all their actions is their
ruling thought.

We have numerous examples of fervent Christians, who have given themselves to God without
measure both in the world and in the cloister.
They have responded to a very special call from
God. But, leaving on one side these individual
calls to Reparation, and speaking of Religious
Life as a whole, we assert that every religious
vocation is necessarily a vocation for Reparation.
It is so of its very nature, whether considered
in general or in detail.

All around we see more and more spiritual
ruins, and labourers needed to restore them all.
Many Christians murmur: " Yes, someone should
attend to this, but why should I trouble?"
Others, though few, humbly and yet resolutely
say: " Yes, someone should attend to it. Why
not I ?" They start at once. They enter
Religion, inspired by the desire to make Reparation ?

Such souls are energetic, they go ahead, in
spite of obstacles. Although friends strive to

keep them back, they enter Religion. *Magister adest et vocat te.* They have heard His call and they obey. What matters if they have to renounce the most sacred ties? With God's help, they are prepared to break them. St. Joan of Arc used to say: "If I had a hundred fathers and mothers, I would leave them." All aspirants to religious life re-echo her words. "A hundred mothers"! How hard it is to leave *one* at such times! Yet in spite of all, they make the sacrifice. A firm determination does not prevent their suffering acutely.

"What are you taking with you into the Convent?" "Nothing. Oh yes, a dozen handkerchiefs to weep to my heart's content." Just then one clings to the merest trifles, and yet goes on.

One says: "I must be off to the King." This is the last word of all who have heard the Divine call: "Go, child of God, go forth," and to whom God gives the courage to respond.

The world knows nothing, sees nothing in such heroism. If it condescends to make any comment, it mutters: "Lunacy!"

"Lunacy!" Well, yes, we accept the impeachment. On one occasion, Abbé Gayraud, then deputy for Finistère, was defending the Religious Congregations in the French Chamber; the question of their expulsion was being discussed and the Abbé was praising Religious and pointing out what greatness of soul it required to renounce the world, act as lightning-conductors for the anger of God and lead a life of self-immolation in union with Jesus Christ. The orator spoke of the Brothers of St. John of God who devote themselves to the service of the insane, of the Little Sisters of the Poor, whose food consists of what is left from the table of the old people they tend, and who, with them, live on what they beg from door to door.

A deputy of the Left, extremely anti-Catholic, exclaimed impatiently: " They are all lunatics !"

" Yes, Monsieur Allemane," quickly retorted the Abbé, drawing himself up to his full height, the better to mark the moral littleness of his interlocutor. " Yes, they are lunatics. Their madness was diagnosed centuries ago by St. Paul as ' the folly ' of the Cross."*

After all, the logic of reason and of faith blended with the logic of the heart seems madness or folly to the world. Yes, folly there is, but not where the world thinks.

The folly of the Cross !

All who are victims of this madness have seen their crucified Saviour passing by. He looked so sad and suffering. They heard His voice murmuring, " Follow Me." Instantly they felt impelled to give themselves to Him alone, to consecrate to Him their hearts, their youthful vigour, all their affections, all their love. Nor did this suffice; they longed to give themselves wholly and for ever to do His will; they desired to suffer with Him and offered to follow Him whither-

* *Folie* in French means " madness " as well as " folly."

soever He should go, not only to Bethania,
Thabor and the Cenacle—that would be simple
enough—but even to the Garden of Olives;
to the Prætorium, where Pilate points Him
out to the rabble, saying, "*Ecce Homo*"; even to
the pillar of the scourging, where He is tortured
and insulted till they reach the Cross on which
He bleeds to death for the expiation of our sins.

Even to the Cross! They had often gazed
at it, but never understood it. Custom prevents
one from noticing. But now for once the Cross
appears quite different, be it the roughly hewn
crucifix of the roadside or the elegant crucifix
hanging over the bed. For the first time one
realises the true meaning of our Lord's words
to Blessed Angela of Foligno: "My love for thee
is not in play!" Not in play indeed! And one
thinks: "There was a cross, a real cross of wood on
a mountain, that showed it once. What a day
was that! Besides all the crosses on which dead
Christs hang, there was once a Cross, on which
the living Jesus hung bleeding, till He died on
it for me, for all men." And thinking of Jerusalem and its blasphemy and ignorance—of the
indifference and hatred of the world—one says:
"How plain it is that if Jesus were to return to
earth, He would be crucified again and even
more quickly than before."

No sooner have we better understood the
Passion of Christ and the world's hatred of Him
than we see that life is altered. We repeat with
Pascal: "Jesus Christ will be in an agony until

80

the end of the world, and during this time we must not sleep."

Sleep forsooth! It ill befits us to sleep when the Divine Master is hanging suffering upon His Cross. Alas! for how many His Passion is of no avail!

When David asked Urias, who had just come from the battle-field, why he had not gone home to sleep, he answered: " My Lord, Joab sleeps in a tent, and am I to lie down in a palace?" After seeing Christ crucified dare we shirk the cross?

To one, who applied for admission into a Carmelite convent, the superioress gave a vivid description of the austerity of the life behind the iron grill. " Is there a crucifix in each cell?" asked the future postulant. " Yes." " Very well, Mother, the rest does not matter; nothing will be too hard." The Saints thought thus.

When St. Philip Neri was dying from sheer exhaustion the doctor ordered him to take beef tea to recruit his strength. They brought it to him and he began to drink it. Presently he left off abruptly, and exclaimed: " Oh, my Jesus! what a difference between me and Thee! Thou wert nailed to the hard wood of the Cross and I am on a comfortable bed. They gave Thee vinegar and gall to drink and I have delicacies. Thou wert surrounded by enemies who insulted Thee and I have kind friends around me, who strive to console me." The contrast made the Saint weep so much that he could not take any more broth, although he was in such need of it.

Wherein lies the great secret of all attraction to a life of Reparation, such as is led by Religious ? In the fact that Jesus was crucified and they embrace the Cross. He suffered, therefore they desire to suffer. Jesus was buffeted and therefore they wish to be despised, ignored, forgotten and even persecuted.

In one of our Lord's apparitions to St. Margaret Mary, He showed her two portraits of Himself. The one represented Him in His Passion, the other in glory. "Which wilt thou choose ?" He asked her. Without hesitation she stretched out her arms to the one representing Him in His sufferings. Yet at the beginning of her Religious Life this Saint had endeavoured to lead a holy life without any suffering. She had carefully sought for a Saint who had not mortified himself and was finally convinced that such a one did not exist.

In the life of the Comtesse d'Hoogworst, Emilie d'Oultremont, foundress of the Institute of Marie Réparatrice, we read of her having a vision, similar to that seen by St. Margaret Mary. When in Rome in 1843 Jesus showed her His Sacred Heart. She says He came to her holding out two crowns, one of roses, the other of thorns. Without speaking or hearing one word she instantly grasped the crown of thorns " with all the love of her heart " as she tells us, adding : " After that I always loved the crown of thorns."

Marie Deluil-Martiny, foundress of the " Filles du Cœur de Jésus," used to say : " If God gave me the choice, I should prefer the Cross without consolation to consolation without the Cross."

How can we explain this strange inclination, this unnatural attraction and inexplicable preference? We must attribute them to souls having discovered, more or less explicitly, that suffering alone can unite them to Him, who is their All. As regards all else, the distance is too great, for on His side there is Infinity, on theirs, nothingness; on His, unspeakable riches; on theirs, unutterable poverty. They could not contend with Him. Where, then, could they find something in common? In this: He has suffered; they can suffer. In all else, He is infinitely above them, for is He not God? But by their suffering they can walk with Him, the Sufferer. On this plane they can meet their God. The road by which He came to them is the road by which they can go to Him. The distance between God and the soul decreases. There is something similar in their lives, and God and the human soul, so different for all else, here have a certain resemblance. The "suffering" soul becomes for God "a helper like unto Himself," one less unworthy henceforth of His choice, His favours and His embrace.

The biographer of St. Lydwine remarks, that within given limits all Christ's devoted servants are called by Him to the work of expiation. Some, it is true, have a vocation that is not directly connected with it, since their special mission is to convert sinners, regenerate monasteries, preach the Gospel to the poor, or they have some secret charge, known to God alone. Yet all these, notwithstanding, are asked to contribute their share of suffering to the common treasury of the Church; all have to give their Master the most genuine proof of their love—namely, that of self-sacrifice. Among these chosen souls there are some who are more particularly called to suffer as propitiation for sin. They are chosen to wear their Master's livery, and these victims include both men and women.

St. Francis Xavier, when dying on the coast of China, murmured continually: " Send me more suffering, Lord." St. John of the Cross had his motto: " To suffer and be despised." In the next chapter we give several beautiful examples of priests who have lived a life of sacrifice. Many others could have been cited, among them those of Père de la Colombière, of Monsieur Olier, of Père Surin and Père Ginhac. Among the laity, Monsieur Dupont, " the holy man of Tours," holds a foremost place.

More generally, however, as Huysmans remarks, it is from among the weaker sex that God chooses His victims of expiation, a fact which this writer explains thus:

" God seems to have set women apart to pay the debt of sin. Men saints have a wider sphere of action and one that attracts attention. They travel all over the world, found or reform Religious Orders, convert the heathen, exercise their ministry in the pulpit by their eloquence.

WHO SHOULD MAKE REPARATION

Woman has a more passive rôle to fulfil: she has not the sacerdotal character and may pass her life in silent suffering on a bed of sickness. The temperament of a woman is more affectionate and devoted, as well as less selfish than a man's. She is likewise more impressionable and susceptible of emotion. Our Lord Himself met with a readier welcome from women; they excel in little and refined attentions, little acts of thoughtful charity such indeed as a man, unless he is a St. Francis of Assisi, overlooks." Further, virgins vowed to celibacy have no outlet for mother-love so instinctive in woman, consequently they lavish all the wealth of their affections upon our Blessed Lord, giving Him the love of a spouse and a mother, for them He is as it were both child and husband. The joys of Bethlehem appeal more to women than to men, whence it follows that they are more ready to respond to the Divine call. Therefore, notwithstanding their changeableness and illusions, the Divine Spouse finds His privileged victims chiefly among women.

St. Teresa used to say: " Let me suffer and die." St. Mary Magdalene de Pazzi amends her saying thus: " Let me suffer and not die."

Marcellina Pauper, a Sister of Charity who offered her life in expiation for the profanations of the Blessed Sacrament and the desecration of the sacred Host, said: " My life is a delicious purgatory, in which the body suffers and the soul rejoices."

THE IDEAL OF REPARATION

Veronica Giuliani, a Poor Clare of the eighteenth century, used to say: " Vive la croix toute seule et toute nue, vive la souffrance " ("Hail to the cross only! Hail to the naked cross! Hail to suffering!"). And Mère Marie du Bourg said: " If sufferings were for sale I would rush to buy them." To these add the testimony of St. Lydwine, in the midst of her terrible pains of body and soul: " I am not to be pitied, for I am happy. If I could obtain my cure by reciting one *Ave Maria*, I would not say it."

Some readers may object: " These heroic souls lived long ago, there are none in our generation." The passage subjoined proves that such an objection is unfounded. It is taken from *Une Religieuse Réparatrice* (Perrin, 1903), to which R. Bazin wrote the Preface. This religious lived in our times. She writes: " I desire to suffer. I will suffer because Jesus has suffered for me and God asks for suffering as an expiation for the sins of the world. I desire suffering because it is the most powerful of all prayers, because it purifies and uplifts the soul. I wish to suffer because therein consists happiness and my soul is hungering for true happiness. *Non mori, sed pati*. I am ready to suffer for a hundred years, if needs be, in order to save souls and glorify God. I need, too, that strength of the soul, that key of Heaven—namely, continual prayer. Prayer unites one to Jesus, and helps one to bear all things for His glory. Prayer is the sister of suffering; they both unite in giving themselves to God and saving the world. Jesus never put them asunder in His Hidden Life, His Passion and when on the Cross."

Simone Denniel, another Religious of Marie Réparatrice, used to say: " The roses for Him, the thorns for me. To be a victim with the Victim, a victim for the Victim, this must sum up my whole life."

In addition to these citations, many others from contemporary sources might have been given—for example, to name only a few, Xavérine de Maistre, Théodelinde Dubouché, Madeleine Ulrich, Thérèse Durnerin, La Mère Marie du Divin Cœur, and Caroline Clément. But besides these saintly women, whose lives have been made public, as a consolation and rebuke to the world, how many in silence and obscurity offer themselves as victims, gladly consenting to do their part towards the work of Reparation, as victims known only to God.

Blessed be these living holocausts, known and unknown, for all the glory they give to the Lord of all, and for the protection with which they surround us, often without our knowledge. " Some people think that with cannons and ammunition our safety is secured. They do not know that side by side with the horrible progress of events on the battle-fields, an inevitable mystical drama is being acted and the purest sacrifice being offered. It is the lamb, not the wolf, that takes away the sin of the world. When seated in the amphitheatre of Ancient Rome, the rhetoricians saw Christians devoured by wild beasts as an interlude; they looked upon the tragedy as an item of the entertainment and nothing more. How astounded they would have been had some prophet foretold that from the blood of those Christians that soaked the arena a new world would arise. If any man had ventured to assert that the catacombs were more to be feared than the Forum, what Roman magistrate would not have deemed him a madman ?" [1]

Thus it is in our days, the same law obtains that those who suffer and expiate in the catacombs are the first and most active labourers in the work of supernatural restoration.

[1] Robert Vallery-Radot.

CHAPTER III

PRIESTS AND REPARATION

GEORGE Goyau, when giving notice of the forthcoming publication of a book entitled *Lettres de Prêtres aux Armées (Priests' Letters to the Armies)*, calls the Holy Mass " the greatest event in the history of humanity," and he adds:

" Daily, the priest brings the effective operation of our Divine Redeemer to bear upon the destinies of the human family. By a supreme act he interweaves the weft of our daily sins with the Divine Ransom; above the chaos of both open and hidden faults he raises the Victim. Our human history is continually being permeated with this Divine sacrifice, a sacrifice both multiple and one. To many this sacred rite is a mere commonplace thing. Nevertheless, through the agency of the priest, they are present at the recurrence of the decisive moment when our guilty world, so justly disinherited, was suddenly put on the way to the plenitude of the supernatural life by the two Mysteries of the Incarnation and the Redemption. God has chosen the priest to perpetuate these two Mysteries, and no human catastrophe can draw him away from this duty, which from the day of his ordination is one, for eternity, with the very life of his soul."

We could not express more briefly the grandeur

and the responsibility of the priesthood. What is the priest? One who carries Christ on through the ages. But Jesus Christ came upon earth to give, to His Eternal Father, a Pontiff, a priest who could adequately make Reparation and Expiation. The priest, therefore, who is charged to prolong, as it were, the rôle of Christ, ought to imitate Him by offering himself with Christ as an evidence of adoration and expiation. The priest who consecrates will therefore be a victim with Jesus. He does not understand his whole ministry if he confines it to the distribution of the Body of Christ, of the word of God, of the forgiveness of Christ, and does not at the same time accept the rôle of victim like his Master, of whom he takes the place and perpetuates the work.

All the years Jesus spent upon earth He was a victim, but He was not satisfied with this, for He had determined to prolong His Sacrifice by the agency of His priests. This He accomplished at the Last Supper, on the eve of His death; hence the Mass sets forth, without the shedding of blood, the immolation of Christ bleeding upon the Cross. Uplifted on Golgotha, Christ between Heaven and earth will be a shield interposed between God's justice and man's sin.

Jesus' mediation will be accepted by God, because of His wounds and His precious blood poured forth. But Jesus is likewise the shield between Heaven and earth, between God's justice and our sins in every Mass. Each " elevation " compensates for our manifold scandals; each uplifting of the Host atones for some decadence of ours, for our falls into sin, because the virtue of His blood and wounds lasts on. There are not two sacrifices, but this is the same as that of the Cross, though set forth differently. This is the formal teaching of the Council of Trent.*

How many of the faithful, who hear Mass, do not seem to have any knowledge of this adorable Mystery! How many use prayers which have no reference whatever to the Mass, though perhaps appropriate for other occasions! How many know the term " Holy Sacrifice," without any conception of the exact truth and stupendous reality with which it corresponds!

Paganism still lingers on here and there. An old rustic used to turn his back to the altar where the Mass was said on the Sunday and pray before an old crucifix—the souvenir of a mission—placed upon one of the pillars. To a Catholic who suggested his turning round since our Lord was on the altar, this peasant replied: " Your God, perhaps, is there; mine is here." Such ignorance is more widespread than is supposed.

But do those who know that the Sacrifice of

* *Una eademque est hostia, idem nunc offerens sacerdotum ministerio, qui seipsum in cruce obtulit, sola offerendi ratione diversa* (Sess. xxii., ch. 2). *In divino hoc sacrificio quod in missa peragitur, idem ille Christus continetur et incruenter immolatur qui in ara crucis semel seipsum cruenter obtulit (Ibid.).*

the Cross and that of the Mass are one and the same know likewise that they are strictly bound to offer themselves to God in union with the self-immolating Victim? This is obligatory, if they would assist at the Holy Sacrifice according to the spirit of the Church and the intentions of our Blessed Lord.

The necessity for the faithful of uniting their sacrifice with that of our Saviour at Mass flows from several considerations, such as: the essential principle of sacrifice and its practice from the earliest ages; the most ancient tradition of the Catholic Church from its foundation; the common teaching of the Father of the Church; the Liturgy of the Mass; certain special ceremonies; and even the matter of the sacramental species, etc.

As far back as we can trace the history of sacrifice as a religious rite, we find that the victim was offered as a substitution for the worshippers, who thereby expressed to God their sentiments of adoration and desire to offer Him some expiation. Now this substitution would merely be a pharisaical and material act. if, by the ministry of the priest and in union with him, the faithful did not offer to God that which the immolation of the victim symbolises—namely, the homage of their piety, and repentance.

When a Jew, under the Old Law, had a sacrifice offered for himself, he had to place his hand upon the victim, as a sign that he united himself with it. In the Mass, we are reminded of this rite, when the priest asks God to accept the oblation which is offered for himself and for all God's family as an act of propitiation. (*H an igitur oblationem servitutis nostræ, sed et cunctæ familiæ tuæ, quæsumus, Domine, ut placatus accipias.*—Canon of the Mass.) In the primitive Church, the Christians gave the bread and wine for the Mass, each contributing his share as a sign of his spiritual participation in the Sacrifice. The Fathers point out that as many grains of wheat and many grapes are employed to produce the bread and wine used in celebrating the Mass, so the multitude of the faithful all united in one body must offer themselves to God. This glorious fundamental doctrine is always the same. Christ is not complete without His Mystical Body, His Oblation is only perfect when we unite ours with it.

Bossuet in his *Exposition of Catholic Doctrine*— a book written for Protestants—explains how Catholics hear Holy Mass. He says: " When we offer Jesus Christ to God, we learn to offer ourselves together with Him to the Divine Majesty, in Him and by Him, as *living victims.*" St. Augustine teaches the same doctrine: " When the Church offers the Body and Blood of Jesus Christ to God, she likewise offers and immolates herself. The true sacrifice of Christians consists in their forming one body with Him " (*De civitate Dei*)

Unfortunately, so few of 'the faithful have any practical knowledge of this sublime truth, which ought to be known and practised by all. If this be true of the Christian, how much more does it apply to the priest! "How gloriously the Church would stand forth if all her children (and we may add, all her priests) understood thus clearly the law of sacrifice. Along with Jesus, in appearance dead, all Christians spiritually sacrificed ought to form one *Victim of adoring Reparation*. Grant, O Lord, that it may be thus with all of us; may it truly be thus. May we be immolated victims with our Eucharistic Lord."*

The priest who really understands what his Mass signifies and who would live up to it fully, should do everything with his Host and nothing apart from Him. *Per Ipsum et cum Ipso et in Ipso.* All by Jesus as Victim, all with Jesus as Victim, all in Jesus as Victim. To live and not to live a crucified life should be to him unthinkable. Undoubtedly, the priest has his failings and defects, they are ever with him, but he will keep his ideal before his eyes notwithstanding and realise that since he offers the Holy Sacrifice, he must be a man of sacrifice.

When Mgr. d'Hulst was made subdeacon his sister sent him a little picture on the back of which was written: " Do not be a priest, without being a victim." This would be an excellent motto for all priests.

We have seen how a true deep knowledge of

* Grimal, *Le Sacerdoce et le Sacrifice de Jésus Christ*, p. 277. Beauchesne, 1911.

94

the Holy Mass should logically lead every Christian, and still more every priest, to offer himself as a victim whenever he hears or celebrates Mass. In like manner, a true and deep knowledge of what *Holy Communion* really is ought to urge every Christian, and still more every priest, to make this offering of himself as a victim every time he receives Holy Communion.

We can look upon the Holy Eucharist from two points of view: as our incorporation with the life of Jesus Christ, and as our incorporation with His death. Both these aspects are equally essential, soundly doctrinal, and have the same claim upon Christian piety.

Yet, in practice, different people give these two points of view a very different reception. Most communicants, when receiving our Lord, look upon it as a means of union with the *life* of our Lord. But how few look upon the Holy Eucharist as a participation in our Lord's Sacrifice and immolation—in a word, in His *death*—as St. Paul explains when speaking of this Sacrament.

As Bossuet says: "Because the death of Jesus is always represented in the Holy Eucharist, the imprint of His death should be stamped upon all the faithful, who ought to offer themselves as victims in union with the Son of God. Such is the power of the Cross, a power that is likewise ever living in the Holy Eucharist." (*Méditations sur l'Evangile:* "Cène.")

St. Paul tells the Christians of Corinth that,

at each Communion, they " shew the death of the Lord till He come " (1 Cor. xi. 26), by which he means them to unite with His immolation, to incorporate themselves with Him in His death. The Author of the *Imitation* develops the same truth: " As I willingly offered Myself to God for thy sins with My hands stretched out upon the Cross and My body naked, so that nothing remained in Me, which was not turned into a sacrifice of divine propitiation, even so *must thou willingly offer thyself to Me daily* in the Mass as a pure and holy oblation, together with all thy powers and affections, as heartily as thou canst " (Bk. iv., ch. viii.).

In another passage, St. Paul asks: " Are not they who eat of the sacrifices, partakers of the altar ?" (1 Cor. x. 18). His meaning is clear if we remember the rites and symbolism of sacrifice in the earliest times. As the Corinthians, to whom he wrote, well knew, to eat of the victim was equivalent to placing oneself upon the altar and taking an active part as victim. To eat of the victim therefore identified the recipient with the victim. St. Paul reminds us that, under the New Law, this likewise holds good. The effect of our receiving the Sacred Host is to give us a participation with the Victim, to unite us intimately with Christ in His immolation, to put us *in communion* with Him—that is to say, to become one with the sacrifice and offer ourselves spiritually with it and consequently to crucify the " flesh with its vices and concupiscences" (Gal. v. 24). This involves giving over to our Blessed Lord our work, sufferings and prayers, our whole selves, that they may be permeated with His spirit of sacrifice. We are told that in the fourth century after having received the Precious Blood in Holy Communion it was the custom to touch the lips still moistened, and with the finger make the sign of the cross on the eyes, ears and forehead. Let us, in virtue of our frequent contact with the Sacred Host, endeavour to purify and sanctify our affections and our thoughts, our heart, eyes and all our members, all we have and are and, to this end, strive to make the necessary sacrifices.

For as Grimal says: " If we desire to reap the fruits of the Holy Sacrifice by Communion without sacrificing ourselves, to be divinised by the sacrifice without immolating ourselves with it, we are simply aiming at living as parasites of the altar and seeking salvation without the cross."

Holy Communion, rightly understood, not only *divinises*, but likewise *immolates:* it cannot do the one without doing the other. Further, rightly understood, it does not consist simply in a treasure received, but must be a treasure given by us; it is not just receiving a sacrifice but giving a sacrifice to God. We cannot worthily receive the Victim of the altar, except on condition of offering ourselves as victims upon the altar in a spirit of adoration and expiation.

On this subject, Mgr. Batiffol says: " Christian piety will always be more attracted by the

Johannine presentment of Holy Communion as a participation in the Divine Life of our blessed Lord, than in the Pauline presentment of it as a participation in His Sacrifice, which will always have a darker aspect."

Will this verdict be revoked one day? May we not hope that when our priests have studied more deeply St. Paul's doctrine on communion with the Sacrifice of Jesus, they will then be better prepared to teach the faithful to offer themselves as victims, whenever they are united with Jesus, the Victim? There are not enough souls willing to make Reparation. Is this by chance, because there are not enough priests who have a deep insight into the mystery of Reparation? How can Christians know it, if those charged to distribute the word of God are ignorant of this doctrine, or if, though conversant theoretically with the grand teaching of St. Paul on Holy Communion, as a participation in the Sacrifice of Christ, they neither live up to it, nor exert themselves with all their energy to spread the knowledge of this truth?

Grimal, in his *Le Sacerdoce et le Sacrifice de Jésus Christ*, writes: "The great lesson of the Sacred Host is the spirit of sacrifice. The Eucharist re-enacts the drama of the Cross. . . . The immediate and necessary effect of Holy Communion is to unite us to Jesus as Victim— that is, to Jesus immolated and immolating."

" Hence, the perfect communicant is he who sees Jesus crucified and enters into His state of being a host. Although the Christian may be in a state of grace and full of pious sentiments, yet if he does not receive our Lord in this spirit of sacrifice, he does not experience the grace of this Sacrament in all its plenitude. He does not understand the meaning of the Host (Victim); it may be owing to his having been taught to esteem rather those virtues connected with the Holy Eucharist, which are of minor importance compared with the one essential thing. If the faithful fail to see the cross ever present and vital on our altars, it may be because they have not been shown it plainly enough."

This same writer continues: " In our sermons on the Eucharist, our great object must be to explain that the Mass is the living Memorial of the death of our Lord, so as to inspire our hearers with *that spirit of immolation, which will make them victims with Jesus in their daily lives.* . . . Let us not fear the reproach of insisting too strongly on the harrowing side of Christianity, on the Passion and on the Christian's offering his life and death as a sacrifice of immolation. Could we do otherwise? Could we modify or veil the chief dogma of the Faith and of our salvation? Let us preach this doctrine in all its plenitude—that the Cross is perpetuated in the Eucharist and ends in Heaven; that the Cross is the portion of the believer and of the communicant, who sacrifices himself by it, that he may live eternally; that the Cross, in all ages and more especially in our times, has a

99

special attraction for privileged souls, for the purest and the noblest, for the lovers of suffering, for the sake of carrying on and continuing the Passion of Jesus. Who can describe the beauty and the fecundity of the Cross when it rules all the faithful ? Who can describe the beauty and fecundity of these chosen souls, who draw their spirit of Sacrifice from the Sacred Host and, immolated with Jesus, are the fragrance and the salvation of our poor earth ?"

" Grant us, O Lord, to be numbered with these souls. Grant that we may help to increase their number by our teaching and direction " (Grimal, *loc. cit.*).

At the present day there is a great increase in devotion to the Blessed Sacrament which Rome favours in every way, encouraging frequent and daily Communion. Let us therefore endeavour to induce all who approach the Altar so often to communicate in the sacrificial spirit, as " hosts " (victims). It is not enough to practise certain mortifications, we must lead lives of mortification, embracing eagerly those numerous occasions of conquering self which occur all day long. We can do even more. In the tabernacles of our altars, Jesus, although alive, is in appearance dead. He permits the priest to handle and distribute Him at will. A holy soul writes as follows: " I think that the greatest act of which the soul is capable is to abandon herself entirely to God together with all she can do, suffer and merit; to allow God to dispose of her as He wills, and to let this donation be known only to Him and to her. This oblation is the soul's highest act, because it gives the greatest glory to Jesus as Victim, because it strips the soul of all she has and is. By this act of homage to Jesus as Victim, the soul enriches Jesus' voluntary poverty by the gift of all the creature can possess and give. . . . This donation of our whole being to God ought to be the habitual state of those who unite with Him frequently in the sacrament of His love, since this self-abandonment is a strict condition as well as the necessary effect of eucharistic union with Jesus. . . . The bitterest sorrow comes to the Sacred Heart from those who are . . . selfish and forget that they are called to complete Its *expiation and intercession* for all men, and hence no longer belong to themselves."

Certainly, many of these would profit more if, instead of communicating to satisfy themselves, they did so to please Him—that is, if losing sight of their interests they sought before all His interests. This is the eucharistic ideal of all communicants who are eager to expiate.

At the outset, a compassionate love is that which predominates in those consecrated to Reparation. They deplore the contempt, indifference and insults offered to God, the ignorance and negligence of men, the persecutions, crimes of the wicked, faults of good people, even of the best, of those even whom our Lord calls "His own," for among His specially chosen there are some unhappy falls. For all these wrongs fervent souls desire to compensate our Lord. Knowing their Master to be so often alone, they visit Him. Since our churches are so empty when daily Mass is said, they will hear as many Masses as possible. In these empty churches, so few approach the altar, therefore they receive the Living Bread daily; thus Reparation leads to the Eucharist.

Then, changing the rôles, the Eucharist leads fervent souls to a spirit of Reparation. The Eucharist is no longer regarded from the outward point of view as of little value from being everywhere in the tabernacle, but the Eucharist is considered and understood as what It really is —namely, as the means of giving Jesus, who is life eternal, hidden as a victim, to all men. The bread and wine are but dead appearances: the faithful communicant is a living appearance of our Lord. What this means in the way of immolation we have pointed out. The altar of sacrifice will always be the great school of sacrifice.

It devolves upon priests to acquire and impart to the best of their power a clear, deep knowledge of the Sacrament, *par excellence*, of reciprocal love.

Now, unless a priest has lost sight of the aspirations of his youth and the obligations of his ordination, he must admit that, with his desire for the priesthood, were mingled ardent dreams of self-sacrifice, and that, on the day of his ordination, when he vowed fidelity to his high calling and binding engagements, he likewise had the set purpose of giving himself up wholly to a life of immolation.

The aspirations of his youth! What ardent desires are stirred up in a boy by reading the lives of St. Francis Xavier, Père Damien, the apostle of the lepers, of the Curé of Ars or of some missionary of Alaska or of Africa! " *Non potero quod isti et istæ?* Can I not imitate what these have done for Christ ?"

When they were quite little their mother trained them to look steadfastly at the crucifix. There are some truths well learnt from a saintly mother. The hearts of children gather that something quite unusual happened on the Cross, something that bound them now and in the future. Jesus there offered Himself for them; they then must offer themselves to Him. What else was to be expected ? In one way or another they imitate the little boy who had heard about the Passion of our Lord; he put his back to the wall and stretching out his little arms in the form of a cross, he asked his nurse to drive nails through his hands and feet. How could he be " so well " when Jesus was " so ill " ?

A child has a true and deep insight into things, especially if he has been brought up at home in the doctrine of self-sacrifice. Some parents are quite careless about this item, but there are others for whom this " item " holds the first place in the education of their children. They teach them to punish themselves, to deprive themselves of what they like. They not only teach them how Jesus suffered for them long ago, but also how the Church is suffering now; they instil into them the truth—though not perhaps explicitly—that God expects something from them when they grow up. We will cite a few examples of such teaching: When the enemies of Religion were making the " Inventory " at a certain church, a Christian father went to protest against this injustice. He took his little boy with him, and lifted him up, that the child might see how Catholics were defending God's rights.

During the French Revolution, Mgr. de Quélen being then a child, his mother took him to visit the Carmelite priests in prison, that he might see how badly they were treated.

Madame Varin felt certain that one of her sons, Joseph, was called to the priesthood, but the boy would not hear of it. Frequently she would call the younger children around her, saying: " Let us say a ' Hail Mary ' for Joseph, who is not following his vocation." When dying on the scaffold, she offered her life that he might no longer resist the Divine call. God heard her prayer, and as a priest Joseph Varin was called to do great things for God.

In addition to his early aspirations the priest has the call of his ordination; he cannot forget that in obeying it, he fully purposed to lead a life of self-immolation. When on that memorable day—so far off perhaps, and yet always so near—

the young aspirant, clothed in his white alb, lay prostrate before the altar, his heart throbbing with emotion, and offered himself to God, did he not intend that, henceforth, his occupation, his one ambition, should be to lead a life of immolation, in union with his crucified Master? The bishop said: " Receive power to offer the Holy Sacrifice"; and then " Thou handlest the paten and the chalice, the instruments of the Sacrifice. Remember they are the instrument of thy sacrifice as well. *Imitamini quod tractatis.* It will be thy charge to handle the Sacred Host. Remember every morning when thou holdest the Host in thy fingers to live as a host thyself. *Quatenus mortis dominicæ mysterium celebrantes, mortificare membra vestra a vitiis et concupiscentiis procuretis.* Christ is dead; thou must lead a life of mortification—a victim along with thy Victim. Thus only canst thou be a true priest: see thou to this. Be it thy chief care to harmonise and synchronise thy life with that of Christ, thy oblation and immolation with His."

Monsieur Olier writes: " I loved to peep into the churches through the half-open doors, and looking at the burning lamps, used to say to myself: ' Happy lights, that are entirely consumed for the glory of God and that ever burn in His honour.'" It is the office of the priest to consume his life thus, since he must be, like our Lord, he who sacrifices and that which is sacrificed. If all Christians are exhorted to offer their bodies " as living sacrifices," how much more is the word meant for priests—priests who say daily: "This is My Body."

True priests give us grand examples of their faithful imitation of Christ as Victim, showing clearly that they looked upon it as the essence of their priesthood.

Abbé Perreyve asked three gifts of God on the day of his ordination: that he might never commit a mortal sin; that he might always remain a humble priest; that he might shed his blood for Jesus Christ. As a symbolic sign of this last request, he celebrated his first Mass vested in red—the colour of blood.

Some time before this generous soul went home to his God, he wrote a meditation on the death of a priest in which he says: "Priests ought to look upon death as one of the functions of their priesthood. It is their last Mass." Following the example of Jesus, the chief use they must make of their bodies—"an essentially priestly use," is to sacrifice them. "They must commence this death by the practice of chastity, continue it by mortification, and end it by their actual death, their last oblation and sacrifice. Like Thee, O Lord, they should prepare for death long beforehand."

A young cleric, in minor orders, of the Seminary of Nevers, who died on April 6, 1907, left the subjoined spiritual will: "I commend my soul to God, in union with our Lord dying on the Cross. I desire like Him, with Him, and in Him, to die a victim. This should be the character of my whole life by my vocation and by duty; may it be that of my last moments. . . . I desire to live in God, detached from myself, so that He may reign absolutely in my soul. Joyfully I offer my Divine Master the salutary sufferings of my last agony and the sacrifice of my life in *Reparation* for the care I have so often taken to avoid suffering and mortification. I offer my life likewise for the Church, for France, for my family."

During the War many, thinking that God would ask of them the supreme sacrifice, offered themselves wholly to God for life and death.

Père Gilbert de Gironde wrote: " How glorious it would be to die young as a priest and like a soldier in a battle, when marching to an attack, while exercising my priestly ministry, perhaps in the act of giving absolution! How grand to shed my blood for the Church, for France, for my friends, for those whose ideal is the same as mine, and also for others, that they may experience the joy of believing !"

Another priest, Abbé Liégeard, from the Grand Séminaire de Lyon and a corporal of the twenty-eighth battalion of Alpine " Chasseurs," offered his life " that the misunderstanding between the people of France and their priests might cease."

Father Frederic Bouvier, S.J., one of the most learned of the historians of religion, said: " I give my life for my companions in arms of the eighty-sixth battalion, that the many upright, good men, whose one defect is living without God and neglecting their faith, may turn to Him."

A seminarist, Abbé Chevolleau, corporal of the 90th Infanterie, wrote this in one of his letters: " Pray that I may abandon myself wholly to God. What matters life, the prospect of offering the Holy Sacrifice, of saving souls later on, if God asks me to offer myself as a ransom to-day ?"

This reminds me of two military chaplains— Père Gabriel Raymond and Abbé de Chabrol— two dear friends, whom I must mention.

The former, a friend of old standing, succeeded me in my little hut in the front line at Artois; the latter I replaced at Tracy-le-val in August, 1916. From the way in which both chiefs and soldiers spoke of their devotedness, it was certain that they could not escape death—they were too daring. We shall never know what acts of heroism these two priests performed : they were so brave, so calm, so unconscious of their merits. Père Raymond was crushed under the roof of a shelter.

A report of an attack thus attests Abbé de Chabrol's courage: " The waves of assailants gave way one after another before God's representative, the chaplain of the division, Abbé de Chabrol, as he stood bravely under fire with his hand raised, making the sign of our redemption and of victory." He was shot down in a fierce engagement, after having offered his life for the redemption of the world and for victory, as Père Raymond and so many others have done.

One more example in conclusion: Père Lenoir, a military chaplain, died on the field of honour on May 9, 1917. He fell a victim to his bravery in succouring the wounded. The Lieutenant-Colonel read to the regiment to which this zealous priest had devoted himself for two and a half years, and for which he had given his life, the following few lines, which were found on his body:

"IN CASE OF DEATH.

"I bid farewell to my beloved children of the 4th Colonial Regiment.

"From the depth of my soul of priest and friend, I implore them to make sure of their eternal salvation by their fidelity to our Lord Jesus Christ and to His Law, by seeking the pardon of their faults, and by uniting themselves to Him in Holy Communion as often as they can.

"I bid them all meet me in Heaven. Also for this intention, I joyfully make the sacrifice of my life to our Divine Master, Jesus Christ, for them.

"Blessed be God! Long live France! Long live the 4th Colonial Regiment!

"P. LENOIR."

Abbé Buathier in his book *The Sacrifice* has this exquisite passage: "Some unknown soul leaves this earth a hundred yards off; no one knows or cares. A few neighbours just make the commonplace remark, ' She is dead.' That is all: there is nothing else for the eyes of the majority.

" But this humble hidden soul had united herself with the Victim of Calvary, she realised the magnitude of the act she was performing. She knew that not only was she satisfying for her own debt of sin, but likewise paying for others—that she was increasing her own merits and bequeathing this treasure to the Church. She knew that by her death she could give life to many and offer them to Jesus: she knew, willed, and longed for all this. Her oblation ascended to Heaven, and in the midst of her agony her sacrifice was consummated; her soul was inundated with that joy which is a foretaste of peace and the beginning of eternal glory.

" For her, as for our crucified Saviour, death had only been the supreme act of love. Men see nothing in it, but angels look on in admiration, and God awards His crown."

Was there not something of this in the deaths we have described ?

Some years ago it was said: " The Church of France needs Saints." The Church of France has had them, she still has them. The examples given prove it, and many more might have been given. Let us hope that, some day, we shall know them all, together with the particulars of their lives. Nevertheless, we must bear in mind that the War, which revealed so much holiness and heroism, created neither the one nor the other.

It was no sudden impulse, no mere chance, which urged these brave Christians to offer their lives as acts of Reparation, in union with their Divine Master. It was, in each case, the result of a long preparation, a volition. It was no improvisation, but a calculated result. It was the daily self-denial in the drab environment of daily life, the practising of mortification, chastity, and zeal, which prepared the soul to offer herself so spontaneously, generously, and totally a victim, and to accept the crucial act of the closing of life.

These brave Christians, let us remember, died, as we have seen, only because they made " a long preparation for death."

PART III

HOW REPARATION SHOULD BE MADE

ALTHOUGH all Christians should make Reparation, they should not all do it in the same way.

The mother of a family might make Reparation, but certainly not in the same manner as a Carmelite.

There are three factors which play their part in deciding to what extent each Christian, individually, can volunteer to walk on the Royal Road of making Reparation. These three factors are:

1. The duties of our state of life.
2. The leadings of grace.
3. The sanction of authority.

Bearing these in mind, we must likewise remember that there are two degrees of self-oblation to a life of Reparation. Taking for granted the acceptance of suffering from the motive of love as the essential principle of Reparation, Christians will be divided in proportion to the measure in which they devote their lives to the Cross.

CHAPTER I

HOW WE CAN MAKE REPARATION BY LEADING A SIMPLE CHRISTIAN LIFE

PEOPLE are too prompt to think that, in order to consecrate themselves to a life of Reparation, they must necessarily live in a cloister, practising silence and the most severe austerities of Christian penance. This is a mistake.

Reparation is not so much the observance of certain fixed *practices* as a *spirit* which adapts itself readily to any mode of life, provided it be truly Christian.

" The *spirit* of Reparation." Hence, before all, it is necessary to bring home to ourselves and to weigh the fact that our Lord was crucified —crucified for us—and that we must help Him; to discover those around us—and how many there are !—who are being lost. This seems a small matter, but how many Christians know nothing about it ! If we live guided by these two great thoughts we possess the spirit of Reparation.

As Chanoine Leroux of Brittany writes: " The life of Reparation is not in itself a particular form of the Christian Life . . ." yet it is not the common life found among all Christians. Why not ? Because, on the one hand, we should try to realise what the Christian ideal really means, and this is rarely done. On the other hand,

" all those who are drawn to seek holiness do not all look at it from this particular point of view " (*La Vie Réparatrice*, Desclée, 1909).

But no sooner do we possess this spirit of Reparation than we see all that it demands of us. We realise that, above all, we must be true to our baptismal vows, and keep the commandments of God and of the Church, not with a fidelity such as the generality of Christians offer God, but with an observance more integral and precise, without bargaining with God or seeking pretexts for escaping from our obligations. To serve God thus loyally in our private, social, and domestic life already opens out wide vistas.

An American author has written a story called *In His Footsteps*. The story commences with a minister who is preaching his Sunday sermon on 1 Pet. ii. 21 : " Unto this are you called, because Christ also suffered for us, leaving you an example, that you should follow his steps." He delivered his sermon, to which his audience listened with their customary respect, but suddenly an old beggar interrupted him by calling out: " What! are you not ashamed ? You dare to sing,

> Jesus, I my cross have taken
> And left all to follow Thee,

and yet live as you do !" Having said this, the beggar fell down dead. There was great consternation among the audience, greater still in the soul of the pastor. On the following Sunday he proposed to his flock that they should form an Association. Each member was to engage seriously for one year to ask himself, before each action: " What would Jesus Christ do in these circumstances were He in my place ?"

A fair number joined the Association—merchants, journalists, politicians, etc. No sooner have they pledged their word than they find that they must change their lives. A certain Mr. Norman, editor of the local newspaper, is one of the members. They bring him an article on the races—three and a half columns of print. He asks himself: " If Christ were the Editor of this journal, would He allow this article to stand as it is?" He decides in the negative, and the article is destroyed. The same fate overtakes other articles, political, commercial, and likewise some advertisements, with the result that the journal ceases to exist.

We see the gist of this story and its exaggerations, but we can profitably retain something of the underlying principle. How perfect would be our Christian life if, like these imaginary personages of this American story, we were to ask ourselves before each action: Were Jesus in my place and in these circumstances, how would He have acted? It is easy to see what a sudden change this would effect in the conduct of individuals, in relations between nations, in the life of families and of society.

A writer dealing with the question of the fall in the birth-rate—a vital matter in these days, and one which convicts many Catholics of having failed in their duty—gives this title to his book: *France Repeopled by Practical Catholics.* The title suggests a scheme while passing a sentence of condemnation.

In no sphere can Reparation be made except by the assistance of true Christians. These must not fail to accomplish their task; they must be Christians to the backbone, fearless and " shameless," as Louis Veuillot explains.

Generous souls will always find numerous occasions of practising their faith to the point of sacrifice. In an earlier chapter we have blamed the tendency, so common with many, to seek the least discomfort possible in their religion. Cardinal Manning writes: " We live in easy times. Who fasts nowadays ? Un-doubtedly the Church is very indulgent. Never-theless, at the present time, the Jews keep strict fasts annually, taking no food from sunrise to sunset, a sharp reproof to us who are disciples of Jesus crucified."

What terrible sufferings some of our soldiers had to endure during the recent War ! For example, the Marine Fusiliers, who, during the famous campaign of Dixmude, had to stand in water for twenty-six days, with no other food than some tins of jam. Doubtless the cause for which they suffered was worth the pain, but is the cause of Christ less noble, though for this we dole out our sacrifices ? Look around ! See what men endure for the world, for fashion.

And we ourselves, what are we doing for souls, for Jesus Christ?

The crucifixes that please us must be artistic, not too harrowing, made of ivory, mounted on velvet. But remember, these are not the true ones. The real crucifix is rough and it hurts.

When Heraclius recovered the Cross from the Persians of Chosroes, who had kept possession of it for fourteen years, desirous of carrying it to the summit of Calvary himself, he put on his most beautiful robes, his diamonds, and his imperial crown. But the Bishop of Jerusalem objected, saying: " No. This cannot be. Do you not see the contrast between your luxurious robes and the bare Cross?" Then the Emperor exchanged his gold and pearls for a hair shirt. The Cross of our Saviour is one that crucifies.

Hence, what a contradiction it is for Christians professing to follow Jesus Christ, to take such pains to avoid the most ordinary penances imposed by the Church! Cardinal Manning asks them with a touch of humour: " Allow me to ask you whether you believe your neighbour when he tells you that he cannot fast, nor keep the prescribed abstinence, that it affects his health, etc.?" And he adds: " I have no scruple in arousing the conscience of some of you, for I am convinced that we are living in an effeminate age, which tends to do away with the gentle severity of the laws of the Church."

Whence it is manifest that we need not seek further. Simply by keeping these commandments strictly, or always in spirit, we have numerous opportunities of offering God very meritorious sufferings and privations, as acts of Reparation.

Secondly, not only must we accept the mortifications imposed by the Church, but likewise those imposed by circumstances, such as reverses of fortune, bad health, bereavements, misfortunes, trials of all kinds. They abound; life is full of them, and is represented by a lyre with seven strings, of which one symbolises joy and six suffering.

Bossuet compares our moments of real happiness to brass-headed nails that stud a door. They appear numerous afar off. Draw them out and you have scarcely a handful. Like the stepping-stones of a ford, our joys are unstable and far apart.

" Who art thou ?" Beatrice asks one who is watching Dante's boat as it glides by. " My name ? Do you not see that I am a weeper ?"

" A weeper." Does not this define every man in this world, at least at certain moments ? Hence, how sad it is to see how few are able to benefit by the tears they shed ! Every one of us, with the total of sufferings which his life involves, has means of acquiring immense merits. Most men make no use of them; they do not trouble about the matter. Instead of utilising their crosses for Heaven and souls, they waste them, reaping no benefit from them, and only find in them occasions of sin, because of their rebellious feelings.

What should we say of a man possessed of a fortune all in gold if, instead of putting it into the Bank as an offering towards the restoration of national historic monuments, he were to stand on a bridge and throw the coins, one by one, into the river ?

Is not our first impulse, when suffering overtakes us, to complain against God ? Our Lord once said to St. Gertrude: " I wish that My friends would not think Me so cruel. They ought to do Me the honour of thinking that it is for their good, their greatest good, that I sometimes force them to serve Me by doing hard tasks, and at their own expense. I wish that, instead of being exasperated by these trials, they would see in them the instruments of My paternal bounty."

The élite of Christians grasp this truth. We give a few examples.

A young religious was attacked by a terrible illness, which carried him off very suddenly. The parents knelt by his corpse. Then followed this dialogue: " We will say the *Te Deum ;* do you agree ?" " Oh, yes, with all my heart."

Ampère had just married and his future appeared bright. Suddenly, his wife was seized with a serious illness. In the depths of his sorrow he had the courage to write this passage: " O my God, I thank Thee. I feel Thou willest that I should live for Thee, that my life should be wholly consecrated to Thee. Wilt Thou take from me all my happiness here below ?

Even so, Lord, Thou art the Master; I have deserved this chastisement. Perhaps Thou wilt yet yield to the pleading of Thy Mercy." What a power there is in strong, deep faith !

A mother heard that her son had been terribly mutilated by a shell. He was a man of great courage, and she wrote this letter about him to a friend : " He suffers a veritable passion in union with our dear Lord. It is wonderful to see this young fellow, crucified, stretched out on his cross of agony, and yet so happy, while suffering a martyrdom every moment. I thank God for linking him with the redeeming sufferings of the Cross. In our grief, we do not understand the mysteries of mercy which these trials conceal, but I believe that in Heaven we shall know the price of these cruel immolations and that our dear invalids are very powerful in God's sight."

This young man intended to become a priest, so his mother adds : " What matters *how* we give, so long as our Lord takes what He wills, and gets all the glory He desires from His poor creature ? . . . If my son cannot be a priest he can be a victim and share the rôle of Christ; who would complain at being treated like the Son of God ?"

Shortly after this man's legs had been amputated, one of his brothers was killed. Still the brave mother shows nothing but brave resignation; she writes : " Only one more victim after so many others. God gave him to us that we might lead him to Heaven. He has reached his goal. It seems so simple, but for us whose faith is so weak, how hard it is !"

How many mothers, sisters, and wives, bereaved by the War, have resolved henceforth to live as mourners. It might have been otherwise had they been courageous enough to transform the sacrifice imposed by God into a sacrifice willingly accepted, if they had said to their Heavenly Father: " Lord, I thank Thee for permitting me thus to share Thy Cross. Father, Thou didst ask for *my boy's* blood, Thou askest for *my* tears; I give Thee all. I should never have had the courage to ask Thee to take my loved one, but since Thou hast taken him, I will be brave enough to say that Thou hast done well. . . . I understand and ratify Thy act. If I cannot say *Alleluia*, at least I will whisper *Amen*. So, it is well."

Another mother, speaking of her son, who had fallen on the battlefield with many others in a glorious and costly campaign, wrote in confidence to a friend: " You know that I gave him up to God at the commencement and now I not only *accept* the sacrifice, but *will* to offer it to God. I place it in His hands." The writer underlined these two words, " accept " and " will."

" My poor heart cannot reconcile itself to its solitude, and it desires ardently to give itself more fully, to offer itself wholly to God." Thus wrote one of the many brave women widowed by the War. O blessed yearning ! May our Lord give it to many souls. She goes on to say that her love, "too human perhaps, will now become more supernatural." This is just what God wants, probably it was why He permitted the trial. Finally she prays "for great courage in offering herself more and more to God."

The excellent nuns who have charge of the Sanatorium of Villepinte have founded for their patients a "Guild of Thanksgiving." One of these young people hesitated about joining, saying: "I fear I shall not be able to say ' Thank you ' to God when I suffer."

The practice of offering ourselves to God as a victim of love and Reparation is an admirable means of overcoming this fear. It would be an excellent practice for so many suffering souls, who are paralysed by the shock of recent events.

St. Jane de Chantal used to say: "The great wealth of the soul is to suffer much lovingly." Real Christians know the truth of this.

Père Ramière writes: "The soul can unite itself to God by prayer, and likewise by work, but that which most intimately unites the soul to God is suffering accepted for God, offered to God, and loved for God. Such suffering is the best of all prayers, the most fruitful of all toil." Père de Poulevoy says much the same: " Undoubtedly the greatest consolation of this life and the greatest resource of our soul is to unite ourselves to Jesus Christ. Yet there is something better, and that is to conform our will to God's Will; to be nailed to the Cross with our Lord or to our Lord by His Cross."

Pascal's admirable prayer *for the time of sickness* is well known. It expresses, better than any prayer we have seen, the desire to utilise to the fullest the trials of bad health, which are so painful and serve so well as acts of Reparation. We give a quotation from it:

"Do not permit me, dear Lord, to contemplate Thy Soul, sorrowful unto death, and Thy Body, the prey of death for my sins, without rejoicing in my sufferings of soul and body. For nothing is baser and yet more common with Christians, including myself, than to live lives of pleasure, whilst Thou art sweating Blood for the expiation of our sins. Take from me, dear Lord, all sadness that is the fruit of inordinate self-love and give me a sadness like unto Thine. May my sufferings appease Thy anger. I ask of Thee neither life nor death, health nor sickness, but I beseech Thee to dispose of my health, sickness, life and death, for Thy glory, for my salvation, for the good of the Church and of Thy Saints."

Elizabeth Leseur, living in the world, chose as one of her mottoes: "Adoration, *Reparation*, Consolation," and wrote in the same strain as Pascal as follows:

"My God, I am and desire to be ever Thine, in suffering or trial, in aridity or joy, in health or sickness, in life or death. I will one thing only, that Thy Will may be done in me, and by me. I pursue and want to pursue one aim only, to procure Thy Glory, by the realisation of Thy good pleasure in me. I offer myself to Thee to be sacrificed wholly, exteriorly and interiorly. I beseech Thee to dispose of me for Thy service and to aid the souls so dear to Thee; to treat me, in so doing, as the commonest and most lifeless of instruments."

All spiritual writers hold that the most profitable crosses are those which God imposes. St. Francis of Sales writes in his characteristic style: " The best crosses are the heaviest, and the heaviest are those which arouse our greatest repugnance, those which we do not choose, the crosses we find in the streets, and better still those we find at home. These are to be preferred to hair shirts, disciplines, fasts, and all other practices of austerity. There is always something of over-nicety in the crosses we choose; because there is something of self in them, they are less crucifying. Humble yourself, therefore, and accept willingly those which are imposed upon you against your will."

But does that mean that all voluntary practices of penance are reserved for the exclusive use of monks and nuns? Many Christians—nay, the greater number—are of this opinion.

There can be no greater mistake. We have cited the passage in which Cardinal Manning exhorts to fidelity to the mortifications enjoined by the Church. To it he adds: " I would go further. Are there any in our days who have the courage to live as the Saints lived? We read and admire their lives. We know how austerely and in what poverty they lived. We praise all that and shudder even to think of it. But what are we able to do? Where are our penances? Do we wear the livery of Christ? While seeking to be placed by the world among its votaries, we profess to be the disciples of Jesus Christ !"

In all Christian countries we find this search for comfort and pleasure—we find Catholics who seek to serve God and Mammon. In our twentieth century, and especially since the War, the world, including Christ's disciples—at least the greater part—seems to live solely for enjoyment of some kind or other.

Pauline Reynolds, when making a retreat, in her humility wrote as follows: " It is no longer possible to dilate the vessel of my heart destined to overflow with the Divine life. The time is over. Yet, by fidelity to grace, I might have cultivated those dispositions which would have obtained for me a thousandfold increase of life throughout eternity. But my will was at fault. *I set limits to trouble I would face.*"

How many Christians, when dying, will have thus to reproach themselves! Yet, if only we put no limits to our generosity in serving God, instead of giving Him a partial fidelity niggardly served out, how greatly could we add to the treasure of merits of the Saints!

Cardinal Manning in his book *The Interior Mission of the Holy Ghost* explains how we can make Reparation. He says: " First, we must promptly follow the inspirations of the Divine Spirit. Secondly, we must proportion our fidelity to the measure of His gifts and graces. We must cease acting meanly and burying the talents confided to us; for a thousand talents we ought to give back ten thousand. Finally, we must serve God with great purity of heart, and by this I mean two things: not only avoiding all that might sully the soul, but likewise *sacrificing* whatever tends to usurp the place of God in our souls."

Hence, it is evident, means of making Reparation are not wanting. What is, then? Souls prepared to utilise these means; souls ready to combat not only greater sins, but their lesser defects. There are wanting souls, who will devote themselves, not to extraordinary practices, but to the steady, resolute performance of monotonous daily tasks and the generous accomplishment of daily trifles, all of which they offer in Reparation. We often aspire to impossible deeds of heroism, but " little things can reveal great love." It is not so difficult to do great things, they carry us away, but the ordinary duties, insignificant and irksome tasks, exact a measure of self-forgetfulness of which few are capable."*

Mgr. de Ségur, with his sound common sense and characteristic subtlety, writes: " Our sanctification is an edifice built up of grains of sand and drops of water. For example, it consists of such trifles as a glance repressed, a word held

* Vallery-Radot, *Le Vase d'Albâtre.*

127

back, a smile checked, a line unfinished, a souvenir stifled, a welcome letter read only once and that rapidly, a natural reaction boldly restrained, a wearisome bore politely endured, a character-istic exhibition, an outburst of irritation sup-pressed at once, refraining from a useless purchase, overcoming fits of depression, tempering nature's transports with the thought of God's Presence in us, overcoming repugnances: what is all this? Just insignificant trifles in the eyes of men who may not see them, but wonderfully clear to Him who dwells within us. Here is what we have to watch closely. Here are both the smallest and greatest proofs of fidelity that will draw down torrents of grace upon the soul."

What miserable creatures we are, seeing that such trifling acts of self-renunciation are the measure of our worth! Yet the fact is undisputed, and no one who has tried to make these acts will contradict Abbé Perrèyve's words, when, speaking from experience, he says: "When we are children, it seems so easy to be a hero or a martyr. But as we advance in life we under-stand the value of a simple act of virtue and that God alone can give us the strength to accom-plish it."

Let us be faithful labourers in performing hidden duties. Who knows but that, during the War, the salvation of some soldier, who fell in the trench or in an assault, was due to his poor suffering grandmother offering her prayers and aches for him. On the battlefield, who can say where the bullet shot by the humblest soldier finds mark?

Do not, dear reader, object: " With what am I to make Reparation? How can I, who am so ordinary and insignificant, do this? Like the prophet, I can only say: *A, a, a, et nescio loqui*—Ah, Ah, Ah, I know not how to speak. I can only sigh and groan and stammer out my inability. Saints? Yes, they can do something, but what can I do?"

Just as you are, you can do a work of justice, and atone for your infidelities by your fidelity to God. You can do even more, you can not only make up for your own spiritual poverty, but you can offer Him your merits in compensation for the defects and sins of others.

We alone, considered in ourselves, can do absolutely nothing. Granted. But we, *plus* the grace of God, obtained by humility and fervent desires, have a strength and value far exceeding our conception.

With what did Jesus nourish 5,000 people in the desert? With five loaves and two fishes. What is the ratio here?

Possibly this saying of one whose whole life was an act of Reparation may carry home a deeper conviction: "It is not of gold, silver, or precious stones that our 'hosts' are made, but of a little bread, which is a common substance and of no value." See the humility of her who thus took courage. Her words are true and contain consolation for each one of us.

CHAPTER II

HOW RELIGIOUS CAN MAKE REPARATION

SIMONE DENNIEL, a member of the Congregation of Marie Reparatrice, just quoted, died very young after suffering for a long time from a painful disease, which doubtless God had sent in answer to her vehement desire to suffer. On November 4, 1910, she wrote: "This morning I made a longer thanksgiving after Communion, because I wanted to tell Jesus again and again that I would be His little victim. I thought that perhaps He was seeking for *victims* and that it would be a great work of zeal to instil into souls the desire to be *victims*. Therefore I will pray and suffer, so that God may increase their number, and raise up true, pure, generous and holy victims."

It is certain that there are souls who are not satisfied with a modicum of suffering. They have for so long contemplated Christ on the Cross, so deeply realised the miseries of mankind, that they cannot do otherwise than wish to become *victims* with Christ for their neighbour and to give themselves to the utmost as a ransom.

In our ordinary language the word " victim " has something derogatory about it. We willingly say " sacrifice," but " victim " has not the same halo. Thus, when we speak of our soldiers' " sacrifices " during the War a glorious picture

130

presents itself to our minds, but when we refer to the " victims " of the War the idea of suffering predominates. Yet these two words denote substantially the same notion: there is no sacrifice without a victim. But while " sacrifice " spells enthusiasm, self-surrender, voluntary immolation, " victim " rather suggests the endurance of a slave, bearing involuntarily some suffering which might more justly be styled an injustice or persecution.

It is regrettable that we have to use a word which leaves an unpleasant impression. We ought to employ it knowing exactly what it means. When we speak of a victim, in connection with Reparation, it does not mean suffering in spite of oneself, but giving oneself up joyfully. For some souls it is not sufficient to practise resignation, acceptance and submission. They seek the Cross; they long to find it, and, having succeeded in their quest, with the Apostle St. Andrew they exclaim: *O bona Crux.* They kiss and embrace it. Notwithstanding the repulsion of their whole being, physical, mental and moral, urged by the love of Christ and of souls, they stretch out their limbs upon the hard, rough beams of the Cross. They offer themselves to be nailed to it. They rejoice to suffer upon the shameful and yet glorious wood.

A fervent religious wrote thus: " Formerly, when our Lord manifested His sufferings to me, I understood Him to say: 'Thou shalt suffer all these.' I knew well that I could never endure His measure of sufferings, but I see that I must suffer in my measure to the full. If I cannot equal His sufferings, I can always fulfil my own." Then she adds: " My chalice is full, how I wish it were larger !"

What a glorious ambition it is to be a victim ! It is a strange ideal, so utterly inexplicable, for those who have no conception of true grandeur. " To be a victim ! What folly !" they exclaim. No, what supreme wisdom ! and how few are capable of understanding its sublimity, because to desire it presupposes so much grace, so many virtues. Yet more souls are capable of this heroism than we might think. All cannot preach, instruct, or write books, but who cannot learn to make the sacrifice of self and to suffer ?

Thus to make the complete oblation of self is the most difficult of all vocations, because it calls for the maximum of self-surrender, yet it is not so inaccessible as it seems, for when we have attained the maximum, the rest matters little. Again, only those whom God especially singles out to devote themselves as " victims " can rise to this degree, but the specially chosen are perhaps more numerous than is supposed.

Let me here remind my readers of what has been said previously, as regards the obligation of consulting our director and weighing the obligations of our state of life, besides yielding to the attraction of grace. It is a very great undertaking to offer oneself as a victim: it needs more than a promise, made in a moment of con-

solation, more than a momentary fervent trans-
port, to face a future that is so formidable. It
does not cost us so much merely to *think* of
suffering, it is quite another thing to *endure* it.
When we kneel in fervent prayer and pain is
seen from afar, it stands out in golden letters;
looked at nearer, we see they are really written
in blood. This does not necessarily involve
bodily martyrdom, but it does include a great
many trials, which disconcert those who made
their oblation with a too ingenuous presumption.

Bearing this in mind, Mgr. d'Hulst states the
exact truth when, writing to a secular, he says:
" The doctrine of Reparation forms the base of
all true interior life." Hence a truly spiritual
life implies the desire to live as a victim, normally
a wish, more or less accentuated, to be a sacrifice
(host). This is as true of the inner life outside the
Religious Orders as of that within them.

As we have already pointed out, it is in Religious
Orders—more especially in those whose one
object is Reparation—that we generally find the
call to be a victim in its normal, though not its
only, centre. There may be fervent souls, living
in the world, leading apparently a wholly secular
life, who are also deeply committed to a life of
reparation.

Mgr. d'Hulst's correspondent was one of these
privileged Christians. In three letters of direction written by him between 1880 and 1885
he summarises his views on Reparation. He says
to her, in a letter dated November 19, 1880:

133

" There is so much to atone for, even—and above all—in the sanctuary and the cloister. God awaits some compensation from those who have received very special graces and profited by them. How grievous are these scandals! Only the thought of Reparation can lessen their bitterness. In taking upon ourselves expiation we resemble Him of whom it is said: *Vere languores nostros ipse tulit.* If we were deeply penetrated by this thought, without binding ourselves to do great penances, should we not at least cheerfully accept the vexations and bitterness of life ?"

He then goes on to explain in detail how Reparation can be made: " We must make atonement by the tears of our heart, by fidelity, patience, deep piety, and love. We must offer our Reparation through the intermediary of Mary and of the Saints, offering God all their merits, their virtues, their love. We must make Reparation by our sufferings, by accepting cheerfully our impotence, spiritual darkness, anguish, weariness, and heaviness of soul. When overtaken by these, let us say: " It is well. I am ready to bear it; the measure is not overflowing. It is better so, better that I should serve as the wood of the holocaust. If I cannot be the priest who sacrifices, nor the victim, I can be the dead wood, burnt by another, destroyed for the glory of God."

Holocaust! This is the limit, there is nothing beyond. A holocaust implies a sacrifice, not a restricted offering, but a total donation, a complete sacrifice, in which the victim is wholly destroyed.

134

Of all the acts of Religion the holocaust is the most perfect sacrifice, the one that is most glorious for God and meritorious for man, because it is the most significant testimony that man can render to God's Sovereign Majesty, the most solemn protestation of His complete dependence upon the absolute power of God.

Père Ramière remarks: " Words are only too often mere sounds pronounced by our lips. God hears only those prayers which come from the heart, and though their language is more sincere than that of the lips, it is nevertheless liable to illusion. True sacrifice consists in the creature giving up self to destruction in honour of God as Creator. Is not this the most perfect way of confessing that God is the principle of his life, the Supreme Arbitrator of his destiny ?

" Sacrifice is not only the witness of sentiments, words, or actions, it is the testimony of death." When sacrifice reaches the limit of the holocaust it can go no farther. Man can offer no more to his Creator. There is nothing beyond total self-immolation.

The great difficulty, however, is not so much giving oneself unreservedly once for all and all at once, so to say, but after having made this wholesale sacrifice, not to retract in detail from the oblation thus made. The practice of making rapines in the holocaust is traditional in the history of the human race, even as regards those who excel in virtue and strength of will. God allows our self-love to assert itself, so that we may always have numerous occasions of meriting. It would be, surely, too easy, too convenient, if it sufficed to make our sacrifice once for all. Over and over again we have to renew this oblation of ourselves and each time integrally. It is this total donation that constitutes our sacrifice and transforms it into a holocaust.

Practically this amounts to abandoning ourselves to God's good pleasure, in imitation of our Blessed Lord, who said: " My meat is to do the will of Him that sent Me, that I may perfect His work " (St. John iv. 34).

Bossuet in his discourse on *L'abandon à Dieu* has some beautiful thoughts on this subject, of which we will cite a few:

" Help me to make this act of abandon, my God, so simple and yet so comprehensive because it gives Thee all that I am, and unites me to all that Thou art."

" This act of self-abandonment includes my whole life, not merely that portion which I pass here upon earth as a captive in exile, but likewise my life in eternity. I place my will in Thy hands, I give back to Thee my liberty of action, Thy gift. I have given all to Thee, keeping back nothing. Man can do no more."

By this act of abandonment to the Will of God we do not remain inactive; on the contrary, we are all the more active since we are more under the impulse of the Spirit and become more energetic in serving God.

136

Self-abandonment to God, as Bossuet explains it, is therefore something totally different from Quietism. In this little work we have frequently quoted him as an additional witness to the orthodoxy of its teaching.

This act of self-oblation further includes such acts as the subjoined. Never doing agreeable things for the pleasure we find in them, but for God. When a choice of two actions presents itself, to choose the more unpleasant. Since Jesus can no longer suffer, to give Him our sufferings even as the sacramental elements give Him their form and appearances. To let Him substitute our sufferings (since He can no longer suffer) for His, so as to satisfy the ardent desire of His Soul to offer sufferings for the Glory of the Blessed Trinity and the salvation of souls. To endeavour to become " *Jesus* " under the appearances of " us."* Within the limits of

* No one has surpassed Huysmans in expressing these thoughts: " Our Saviour cannot now suffer in person. If He wants to bear suffering on earth, He can only do it through the Church in the members of His mystical body. The practisers of reparation, renewing the horrors of Calvary, nailing themselves to the bare blank Cross of Jesus, are after a fashion His counterparts. Nay more, they, and they alone, render to Almighty God something that He lacks, the possibility of continuing to suffer for us. They satiate the desire that survived His death, for it is as infinite as the love from which it springs." They " give the mysterious Needy One the alms of their tears and restore to Him a joy that He has renounced, the joy of being a holocaust " (*Vie de Ste Lidwine*, p. 101).

discretion and obedience to desire and seek mortification in the little details of life, as a preparation for greater sufferings, should it please God to impose them.

Such are the sublime aspirations of some privileged souls. Joyfully they endeavour to live up to this ideal, each according to her special spiritual attraction and distinctive form of piety.

A word in passing on the " Heroic Act " may fittingly find place here. Some devout Christians make the oblation of all their merits to be applied just as God thinks fit, or for the deliverance of souls from Purgatory. They offer all the indulgences they may gain, and all that may be gained for their intention after their decease, for the release of the holy souls.

Another generous act is to make a vow always to do that which is most perfect. Those who make this vow should have sound common sense, a well-balanced judgment, and the sanction of obedience. Otherwise it might be a fruitful source of scruples and eccentric actions. Here, more than anywhere, souls need " a mind that calculates and a heart that does not calculate." Both are necessary, but the latter is a *sine qua non*.

Others, again, go so far as to engage themselves by a solemn vow to live as victims of Reparation. In the Constitutions of the Benedictines of Perpetual Adoration, which have received the approbation of the Holy See, we read: *Voves et* *promitto . . . omni studio servare perpetuam SS^t* *S^t altaris adorationem et cultum, uti victima gloriæ ipsius immolata* (C. lviii., § 23)—" I vow and promise with all diligence to keep up the Perpetual Adoration and worship of the most Holy Sacrament of the Altar, as a victim immolated to Its glory." Hence, this solemn consecration as victim for the glory of God has the formal approbation of the Church. Pius X., by a decree dated December 16th, 1908, and a brief of July, 1909, accorded a monthly indulgence to those priests who, under given conditions, take a vow as priests to make Reparation.

But vows of this kind are as difficult to keep as the vow always to choose the most perfect line of action, which the Church speaks of as *arduum* and *arduissimum* in the office for the feasts of St. Andrew Avellino and St. Jane de Chantal respectively. Whence it is clear neither is to be recommended, nor made without wisdom and discretion, prudence and authorization. These are absolutely necessary conditions.

We do not propose to explain this vow of Reparation in detail, we leave it to those skilled directors to whom it more particularly appertains and who can deal with it competently. Hence, we pass it over with a brief explanation of the foundation and subject-matter of this vow.

Those who desire to make this solemn promise must commence by defining what they intend it to include. These promises may embrace various degrees, but, speaking generally, they can be

139

divided into two classes. The first comprehends all those sufferings which are brought about *by the ordinary Providence of God*—sufferings which He has foreordained from eternity. Those who accept these willingly are really, " victims " in the hands of God, and they offer Him a very perfect oblation.

Secondly, those fervent souls—not content with these ordinary sacrifices, and desiring to immolate themselves more completely—who beseech God to send them additional sufferings, *as a supplement to the former.* These include sufferings of body, mind and soul, or even a premature death.

How far is this second and higher degree (1) possible, (2) praiseworthy ? These questions must be discussed with extreme caution and great attention, for in such a delicate matter there is a real danger of illusions. As great generosity may lead to temerity, we must exercise all the more prudence and apply more rigorously the rules for " the discernment of spirits."

Of course it is not necessary to make either of these vows in order to lead a life of Reparation. They may crown such a life, but are not necessarily its foundation. They mark a maximum, something as it were over the line.

It is a great victory for God that there are souls in this world who desire sufferings with as much avidity as the greater number of men seek pleasures. It seems as though God rejoices in the fact of their existence, by fulfilling willingly their hearts' desires. For He Himself has given them this thirst. When God wants to fill a heart He begins by emptying it. Whereas all around them have no room within for such yearnings, they are tormented with a thirst to satisfy them to infinity.

First of all, they cannot let our Lord suffer alone upon the Cross, they must alleviate His Sufferings by sharing them. They long to wipe His bloodstained brow, to expiate the blows of the hammer when the nails were driven into His sacred feet and hands, the purple furrows of the lash, by their voluntary and loving oblation. The back of Christ's Cross is empty; there they will seek to be nailed, eager for one thing only, to be crucified in His exact likeness.

They take the advice of St. Catherine of Siena to the letter, which is as follows: " Let the tree of the Cross be planted in your heart and in your soul. Become like unto Jesus crucified. Hide yourself in His sacred Wounds, bathe yourself in the Blood of Jesus crucified, permeate and clothe yourself with Jesus crucified, satiate yourself with opprobrium in suffering for the love of Jesus crucified."

A saintly soul, whose Life will, we trust, soon be published, made this candid avowal to her director. She wrote: " We would like sometimes to sing the mercies of the Lord, be it ever so little, but this poor lyre vibrates too much, owing to the density of the materials of which it is made: I can scarcely make any use of it. I began to write

141

to you a few days ago, but was obliged to stop. The first note gave out such a volume of sound, that a second would have snapped the cord.

"My body is too small for my soul and my heart cannot contain my love for Him. . . . I can rarely speak as openly with you as I have done this evening, and I have only been able to do so by looking away from Him."

It is related of a religious that, by a special grace of God, she was so overcome with sorrow at the thought of our Lord on the Cross, that she had made a resolution not to look at the crucifix. It chanced that, in order to go to the refectory, she had to pass by a large crucifix fastened to the wall. One day she raised her eyes to it, and contemplating the bleeding Wounds, fell fainting to the ground.

Exaltation! sensationalism! you exclaim. Be it so. But, after all, which is most extraordinary? The one who cannot look at the Cross without suffering, or all who contemplate it without feeling any grief whatever. Unlike us, Saints cannot look upon the Divine immolation with indifference. Those strange beings, Saints, suffer when they see our Lord suffer. Alphonsus Rodriguez, a saintly Jesuit lay brother, wrote: "It seems to me that were this suffering of compassion to be prolonged, no form of torment, however horrible, could be compared with it, for this depth of sorrow of soul resembles that of our Lord in Gethsemani, when He prayed saying: " My soul is sorrowful, even unto death." It was then that He sweated blood. This holy porter of the College of Majorca offered himself to endure all possible sufferings, even those of the lost, in order to obtain from God that men might cease to offend Him and that no soul might henceforth be lost.

In the *Acta Sanctorum* in the Life of St. Bridget of Sweden, whose feast is kept on October 8th, we read as follows: " When very young, she heard a sermon on the Passion. She was so impressed by it that she imprinted these sorrowful scenes upon the tablet of her heart. The following night she had a vision of our Lord upon the Cross and He said to her: ' This is the treatment I have received.' With her childish simplicity, she asked: ' Lord, who has done that to you?' Jesus replied: ' All those who despise Me and are insensible to My love.' From this moment St. Bridget was so touched by the Passion of our Saviour that she could not help thinking of it continually, always shedding bitter tears over Jesus' sufferings."

This exterior proof of sympathy with our Lord's sorrows is a special gift of God, one of His choicest. Nevertheless, this does not cancel what we said above—namely, that the total abstention from all outward tokens of sympathy proves great indifference and inconceivable ingratitude on the part of men.

If only the Crucifixion of Jesus did some good! He is there, the Divine Mediator, suspended between Heaven and earth, so mangled, so suffering, and so stupendously ignored.

How can we furnish the tribute of glory which is due to God and refused Him by man? By loving Him?

Alas! a poor human word, and it represents a still poorer thing. With what can we love? With our wretched human heart? For the heart of man to love God seems a derision, mere irony. That which is the weakest, can it love that which is greatest? Can we, so ungenerous, love Him who has given Himself without measure? His generosity is proved by the manger, the Cross, Holy Mass, the Sacraments, the Church. He gives all; how can we who limit and begrudge our gifts offer Him anything? Can we whose love is feeble, so unworthy of the name, love Him who is love itself? No, Lord, we cannot compete with Thee.

What a conflict! To enter the lists with one who wields the infinite, this thought inevitably rends and tortures the soul. We long to give and have not the wherewithal. We would fain give much and our hands are empty. To Him who is All, we must ever give so little.

Assuredly, it is not necessary to possess much in order to give much. He who gives all he possesses, however little it be, certainly gives much.

Yet, herein is another source of spiritual anguish: a continual torment, because one is conscious that one does not give wholly to God the little one has. We know ourselves and cannot but admit our daily shortcomings. These may be trifles, but still how hateful it is to show the least lack of feeling in one's love of God. Hence, what should lessen her suffering only increases it. One longs to console the Master, by offering oneself wholly to Him, but is conscious of numerous evasions, acts of meanness and self-love. St. Francis of Sales wittily tells us we shall not get rid of this feeling until a quarter of an hour after death. It is just this that overwhelms one. We have to serve God, who merits all; we have so little to give Him and this little is not fully given up.

God torments Saints with this constant anguish. Their desires continually grow stronger, and He only puts this consuming flame in their hearts that He may contemplate their great magnanimity with pleasure, amidst all the pettinesses that He hates.

Sister Teresa, of the Infant Jesus, once said to our Lord: " I offer myself to Thee as a victim, a holocaust to Thy merciful love, that I may live in an act of perfect love. I pray Thee, consume me unceasingly; let the torrents of infinite tenderness that overflow Thy Soul pass into mine, so that I may be a martyr of love, O my God. . . . O, my Beloved, with every beat of my heart, I renew this offering to Thee an infinite number of times, until earth's shadows shall have passed away and face to face in Eternity I can tell Thee my love."

In a meditation in which St. Mary Magdalene de Pazzi received great spiritual illumination from God, she speaks thus of St. Aloysius Gonzaga: " Who can ever explain the priceless value of interior acts and the reward they merit ! There is no comparison between what appears without and what takes place within. St. Aloysius, all his life long, thirsted after the interior inspirations which the Word breathed into his soul. He was an unknown martyr, for all who love Thee, my God, all who know how great and infinitely lovable Thou art, suffer a cruel martyrdom on seeing that they do not love Thee as they would wish, and that instead of loving Thee, so many continually offend Thee."

It would be some consolation to those who thirst for God, at last to find Him and hold Him in a loving embrace. . . . But alas ! as we follow after God, He hides Himself. True, there is the Holy Eucharist, but the Real Presence does not last always; it is so mysterious: *Visus, tactus, gustus, in te fallitur.* There is sanctifying grace, but the continual Presence of God in the soul does not always ensure the presence of the soul in herself.

We are continually away from ourselves. Our frequent and trivial daily cares carry us far from this precious centre where, by sanctifying grace, " The Three "—Father, Son and Holy Ghost—always dwell. God is present *in* us: we are there not at all—or so little.

Then there is prayer, but even so we must be content with faith, while we desire possession, with the reflection instead of the gift, with the image in the " glass " instead of the " face to face."

We want to be like unto Jesus, and yet how utterly far away He seems, how hidden, how hard to realise. Then we must add those terrible spiritual trials of aridity, when the Divine Master seems so far off and dim that we can scarcely recognise Him and cry out with the Apostles on the lake: *Phantasma est !*—" It is an apparition."

Yet Jesus knows we have left all to follow Him. Marie de la Bouillerie, who became a religious of the Congregation of the Sacred Heart, speaking of her mother, said: " I will never leave her for a man." But the religious leaves her mother because she knows that Jesus was more than man. She says resolutely to Him: " I will follow Thee. Where dwellest Thou ? " He replies: " Wilt Thou follow Me ? Come then." She sets out for the Promised Land, knowing that the road is long, and that it leads through the desert. What matters it ? After a weary march, she thinks she has reached her Master's abode, the King's palace—she knocks at the door like the child who once clambered up on to the altar, knocked at the door of the tabernacle and called out: " Lord, are You there ? " and got no answer from within. So for her, too, the Tabernacle door remains closed. God does not reveal Himself.

Deus absconditus—"He is a hidden God." He crucifies and remains hidden, unspeakably mysterious and unapproachable! There we stay knowing that He is within and could open, but prefers to wait. Thus was it with St. Mary Magdalene at the tomb on Easter morning. She sets out at dawn with her humble offering, a few spices—it is all she can offer—and she hurries on her mission of love. She reaches the garden and enters the tomb. The tomb is empty—there is an angel, the grave clothes, some traces of Him—but not the Master! Yet " He " is the one she wants; not just the word of an angel, but a word from Him, His own lips; not merely a relic of His showing He was there just now; but *Him*, there in fact, now, plain to all of us. " Art thou here, O Lord ? " He is not far off. He is always close to those that seek Him.

" Thou wouldst not seek Me, hadst thou not already found Me." Pascal places these words on our Lord's lips, and they express a great truth. Those who seek in earnest and cry out: " Lord, where art Thou ? " are no longer on the way—they have reached the end. While Mary Magdalene was asking for Him, the Master was there, standing in front of her. It was He Himself though He showed Himself as usual, in a disguise, as a gardener, and she did not recognise Him: " Tell me where He is. Wherever He is, let me go to find Him."

If the Lord manifested Himself openly, He would satisfy the soul's desire, but not His own.

He takes pleasure in the spiritual thirst of fervent souls. He is like a mother who hides for her child to find her. " God desires nothing so much as to be desired," as St. Augustine says. That is why His wise action tortures us, but affords Him such pleasure. *Deus absconditus.* God hides Himself, and this is why His lovers suffer so much.

Religious have left all for God, that they may be united with Him and yet, in spite of all their desires and efforts, they find they can never possess Him and be wholly His. With the spouse in the Canticles, they exclaim: *Fasciculus myrrhæ dilectus meus*—" A bundle of myrrh is my Beloved." In the bitterness of their myrrh, God finds a sweet perfume of the greatest love.

Thus He could not long withstand Mary Magdalene's entreaties. Familiarly, as of old, He pronounces her name, " Mary !" Nor can He resist souls that seek Him. At times He allows them to see Him as in a flash. They feel that they need only throw themselves at His feet, and stretch out their hands to lay hold of Him for ever ! Then He speaks: *Noli me tangere.* On hearing these words " Touch Me not," their sorrow is at its sharpest. Is this to be the sole reward of their love? Has it counted for no more? " Lord, take away my heart's desire, or have mercy on me," they cry. But then especially He refuses to treat them otherwise. He wishes to deepen their inward yearnings, and hence He bids them wait with patience, and veils the reality of mercy under the form of ruthlessness. It is

related that He once said to Pauline Reynolds:
" My hour has not yet come. Be patient, in a short
time you will see Me." " Do You speak thus to
a soul that loves ?" she answered; to which our
Lord replied: " Yes, I speak thus to one who
loves because I love. Trust Me implicitly."

Amidst the sufferings which spring from a soul's
insatiable desire to give something, even much,
to God, He provides her with means of showing
herself more equal to her high ideals. That self-
sacrifice spells suffering, the soul is convinced.
She is unhappy precisely because her offering to
God has cost too little.

Then, God sends great crosses, such as aridity,
illness, false friends, persecution, failures, and many
other kinds of excruciating suffering. Our Lord
is never at a loss for crosses. His workshop is
full of them. At Nazareth He apparently
spent all His time making crosses of various sizes
and kinds of wood.

This is how God acts: To slake a soul's thirst
for sacrifice He sends suffering. He fills the full
cup of suffering by making it overflow, and the
fresh influx of bitterness results in the greatest
happiness. Were we not accustomed to be so
continually baffled by God's mysterious dealings
with man, how amazed we should be at the
strange paradox, by which our loving God imposes
such great sufferings on those who are generous
enough to offer themselves as holocausts.

St. Lydwine, as we have previously said, exclaimed in the midst of her pain: "Do not pity me, I am happy," and all who walk in her footsteps re-echo her sentiments. Her biographer takes these words as his text in one of the finest passages ever written on suffering. This is the substance of his remarks: Victims suffer most of all and yet are the happiest of all. To offer oneself for a holocaust is to offer oneself for happiness, for Jesus owes it to Himself to repay in peace and joy that which has been sacrificed for Him so generously. This is the experience of all eminent self-immolators. God compensates them so abundantly for their sacrifices that they exclaim: "Dear Lord, what a blundering bargain. I meant to suffer and expiate, and I have nothing but happiness." A soul says to Jesus: "Let me be nailed to Thy Cross by Thee, O Lord." Jesus grants the petition. He drives in the nails; then seeing the blood flow and the victim break down, His heart breaks: He cannot go on. He stops, draws near and fills the void wrought by suffering with joy, so that the soul begs to be spared joy, as earnestly as others beg to be spared sorrow. Yet she goes on suffering, but her suffering is her happiness or rather, while still feeling her suffering, it is so full of divine gladness that she would not be relieved of the suffering for anything in the world. She must have it to provide fuel for the fire of sacrifice; and God trains the soul with alternate gladness and grief, each making the way for the other. Yet after all, suffering is swallowed up in joy;

and the soul's unstifled sobs break forth like " hymns," as Bauthier finely says.

Abbé Perrèyve, a writer who excels in understanding and explaining the paradox of suffering and joy intermingling or balancing one with the other, writes: " How comes it, Lord, that no sooner have I set out on the way of the Cross than I hear such sweet consoling words ?" No sooner has Jesus said: " If any one will come after Me, let him take up his cross," than He adds : " My yoke is sweet and My burden is light." The Abbé continues: " I have only just commenced my sacrifice when Thou givest me consolation; no sooner have I taken up my cross than I feel Thy Divine hand lessening its weight."

" O Jesus, Thou who orderest the sacrifices that are needed, and yet dost ever diminish their pain by Thy tender love, Thou dost command us to renounce self, and when we practise detachment from creatures, Thou givest us far more treasures than we have given up. Thou commandest us to take up our cross daily, if we would follow Thee, and then dost exchange it for a yoke that is sweet and a burden that is light. Thou art often so pleased with the least proof of our goodwill, and dost reward our feeble efforts with unutterable consolations. Henceforth, I will not be afraid of Thee nor of Thy Gospel, nor will I tremble on hearing the word ' cross.' I know that the Cross contains the secret of all great consolations; and real succour in the pathway of life, where inevitably we must suffer. I draw near with confidence to the Cross; kneeling before it, I would find fresh graces of strength and patience by meditating on Thy Passion. Dear generous Master, do not refuse me this gift; receive me in the ranks of Thy faithful Disciples, who, following Thee even to Calvary, find courage to endure their trials, and grace to exchange earth's bitter sorrows for boundless wealth."

Can we do better than close this chapter with such a beautiful, fervent, confiding and humble prayer?

Humility is the characteristic that finally sets its hallowing seal upon the true spirit of Reparation. All who resolve to devote themselves with Christ, to redeem the world by suffering, tremble as they do so, knowing their utter helplessness. They know that, left to themselves, the least touch of suffering would put them to flight. Those who offer themselves with the wine of the sacrifice know well that they are but drops of water. It is ever the most generous who realise most fully the utter insignificance of their gifts.

CONCLUSION

WE have not tried to write an exhaustive or learned treatise on Reparation, but to explain simply the theological and dogmatic foundation upon which it rests, and the proper place in Christian life and thought of this *Ideal*.

At the present moment many seem to be drawn towards it, but because they do not clearly understand in what it consists, they hesitate, fumble about, give up, or go off on the wrong scent. These few pages seek to awaken some souls, and to help those already awake, but needing enlightenment, by sketching out the first principles.

Undoubtedly, in such a matter, a monograph or a living example is better than a booklet. This is why we have so frequently quoted from *lives*. However, a brief outline of the theory may be useful and serve as an attraction and a landmark. Afterwards, the perusal of deeper treatises, the advice of a skilled director, and the grace of the Holy Spirit, may complete the work of enlightenment, conviction and stimulation.

During the recent War, along the roads leading to the battle front, here and there, you came across notice-boards, on which were roughly scrawled names of places and arrows. They pointed the way to some definite goal. These pages are

simply meant to say: To SELF-SACRIFICE—
" Follow the Way of Reparation." They tell
you the road to the goal from afar, not what
you will find when you get there.

Just as only those who lived in the trenches
during the War know what kind of life our
soldiers lived, and all that happened there, and
alone can speak of it with authority, whether or
no they are listened to or believed in, so only
those who have been taught by God, either by
personal experience or by contact with privileged
souls, can adequately instruct others in the
complete overthrow of self-love, in self-anni-
hilation, and in the blood-dyed festivities of the
total giving over of self to God.

This accounts for the particular form of this
book, for its incomplete and cursory nature.
It does not befit us to sound depths which God
reserves to Himself, to search into " the King's
secret " and explain how He communicates Himself to those whom He calls to give up all for
Him. To do that presupposes authority, practical
asceticism, and mystical experience, and something else which the author does not possess.
A blind man does not describe light.

We are only too conscious of how far this little
book falls short of expectation. But, however
imperfect this modest work be, God can utilise
it for His glory, if He so wills. Sometimes He
makes use of the most inadequate means to
produce the results He desires.

In September, 1917, during the War, two

soldiers were on leave at Hersin-Coupigny in Pas-de-Calais. They decided to return to their native village to look for their savings, which they had buried before leaving for the campaign. One found his money, the other nothing whatever. Before returning they went to see their old church. Alas! it was in ruins, only a cast-iron crucifix that had been fastened to the wall remained erect. One of the soldiers reverently kissed it, in presence of a group of Canadian comrades who applauded heartily. Then, turning to his companion, he said: " You have found your treasure and now I have found mine. I will take it away." They took the heavy cross, carried it over the beaten tracks, and through underground passages, and at last, covered with mud and dripping with perspiration, they reached Hersin and there placed the cross of their church in safety.

To *find* the Cross, not that of a church in ruins and among the débris, but our Lord's Cross planted on Calvary, might seem an easy task. Yet it is not. As Mgr. d'Hulst truthfully says when speaking of the Feast of the Finding of the Holy Cross: " It is a great discovery. For a long time we have had thieves' crosses that dishonour, but the great revelation is the Cross of Jesus. How many souls have yet to find it !"

Yes, souls must first find the Cross, but this does not suffice. They must clasp the Cross in their arms. The Canadians applauded their brave comrade. The world will not understand the true Christian's love of the Cross. What matters it?

Having taken up their Cross, they must place it resolutely upon their shoulders. They will find their narrow paths, their subterranean passages, and obstacles which will make them stumble and fall. The path is rough, the road long. They will often be tempted to throw down their burden, to rid themselves of its weight and ease their aching limbs. Then the Master asks: " Wilt thou leave Me there? Is there no one who will, like Simon and Veronica, take charge of my Cross and help Me?" Will none come forward? Are our Master's words true?

One day, while Blessed Angela of Foligno was hearing Mass, our Lord gave her a great realisation of the sufferings of Jesus on the Cross. She writes: " I heard Him bless the unselfish who imitated His Passion and took pity on Him. He said: ' May the hand of My Father bless you, who have shared and wept over My Passion. You whom I have ransomed from hell by My terrible sufferings have taken pity on Me. May His blessing rest on the faithful who have remembered My Passion and kept the memory of it in their hearts, for they have offered to their Lord in His desolation the sacred hospitality of their love.

" I was naked upon the Cross, I hungered and thirsted, and you pitied Me. I bless you for your work of mercy. In your last moments, I will welcome you, saying: Come, ye blessed of

My Father, for I hungered and you dealt out to Me the bread of your compassion. If, hanging upon the Cross, I prayed for My executioners, what shall I say of you who have served Me so faithfully when I come in glory to judge the world? I cannot express the love I feel for all hearts full of pity."

More than ever, at the present time, Jesus asks for " devoted souls, ready to imitate His Passion and to pity Him."

May the Divine Master lead at least a few of the readers of these pages to enrol themselves in the cohort of the " devoted," and grant them the generous desire to join the " pitiful in heart."

Who is willing?

" Here am I, Lord."

Printed in England.

CPSIA information can be obtained
at www.ICGtesting.com
Printed in the USA
BVHW040206040121
596922BV00015B/590